Securing a Safer Blood Supply: Two Views

Securing a Safer Blood Supply:

Two Views

Ross D. Eckert

Edward L. Wallace

American Enterprise Institute for Public Policy Research
Washington and London

Library of Congress Cataloging in Publication Data.
Eckert, Ross D.
    Securing a safer blood supply.
    (AEI studies, 416)
    Contents: Blood, money, and monopoly / Ross D.
Eckert—The case for national blood policy / Edward L.
Wallace. 1. Blood—Transfusion—Economic aspects. 2. Blood—
Transfusion—Complications and sequelae. 3. Blood
donors—Diseases. 4. Blood banks—Government policy—
United States. I. Wallace, Edward L. II. Title.
III. Series. [DNLM: 1. Blood Banks. 2. Blood Donors.
WH 23 E19s]
RM171.E27 1985   362.1'783   85–1344

ISBN 0-8447-3571-X
ISBN 0-8447-3572-8 (pbk.)

AEI Studies 416

1 3 5 7 9 10 8 6 4 2

Printed in the United States of America

Contents

The Case for National Blood Policy
Edward L. Wallace

Foreword

The authors of the two studies presented in this volume—Ross D. Eckert of Claremont McKenna College and Edward L. Wallace of the State University of New York at Buffalo—are deeply committed to the goal of enhancing the quality of our blood supply. Their views on how this goal can best be attained differ sharply, however, and the American Enterprise Institute is delighted to publish these two articulate, policy-relevant studies of how the blood services system should be structured.

Eckert argues that the quality of our blood supply is diminished by an unnecessarily large volunteer donor pool that leads to inadequate screening for the risk factors associated with transfusion-related diseases. He criticizes current collection procedures and advocates a smaller, more tightly screened pool of donors who could receive cash payments to encourage regular donation. Eckert further argues that the lack of competition in most cities for the American National Red Cross or other blood services has been counterproductive to the attainment of a safer blood supply.

Wallace defends the current volunteer donor system and the role of the American Red Cross, arguing that the system has brought about a marked decline in the incidence of transfusion-related disease. He supports the elimination of commercial services and paid donors and opposes their reentry. The Red Cross has not, he argues, been guided by monopolistic intent, as Eckert asserts; it merits praise for undertaking a nationwide effort to help promote and maintain an adequate supply of high-quality blood.

The views expressed by Eckert and Wallace contribute timely information to an issue of growing importance—the danger of illness transmitted through blood transfusion. As the authors indicate, acquired immune deficiency syndrome (AIDS), though tragic and the subject of a great deal of media attention during the past two years, results in far less transfusion-related mortality and morbidity than hepatitis. Given our limited ability in blood samples, to identify much less cure, AIDS and new strains of the hepatitis virus, transfusion-related disease will become an increasingly important issue in public health policy. The authors provide important information on the scope and nature of the problem along with their presentation of alternative solutions.

This volume reflects a continued interest in blood quality issues at AEI's Center for Health Policy Research. In 1976 the center held a conference on blood policy, which resulted in the 1977 publication *Blood Policy: Issues and Alternatives*, edited by David B. Johnson. On a broader scale, the book meshes well with AEI's efforts to help determine the appropriate roles of the public, private, and nonprofit sectors in meeting the health care needs of our society.

WILLIAM J. BAROODY, JR.
President
American Enterprise Institute

Blood, Money, and Monopoly

Ross D. Eckert

Acknowledgments

This project covered the span between fall 1979 and summer 1984. Over half the financial support was provided by the Center for the Study of Law Structures of Claremont McKenna College under a grant from the John M. Olin Foundation. Additional grants were made by the Wohlford Fund and the Faculty Research and Development Fund of Claremont McKenna College, the Claremont Center for Economic Policy Studies of the Claremont Graduate School, and the Haynes Foundation. Thomas M. Asher and Carol K. Kasper suggested sources and helped with technical materials. Gordon Bjork, Thomas E. Borcherding, Yale Brozen, Enid F. Eckert, Susan K. Feigenbaum, George W. Hilton, William T. Jones, Marvin Kosters, Charles A. Lofgren, Jack A. Meyer, Rodney T. Smith, Michael B. Sutton, and Colin Wright commented on drafts. James D. Hess performed the statistical calculations in chapter 2. David Ransom organized my word-processing system, and Ellen M. Raine and Erin McElrath were my research assistants. Joel Menges helped to coordinate the publication process at AEI. The American Association of Blood Banks, the American Blood Commission, the American Blood Resources Association, and the American National Red Cross provided source material. I am grateful to all these people and institutions for their help. Responsibility for the views expressed and for remaining errors is mine alone.

2

1
Introduction

About 3 million Americans each year—and 95 percent of the U.S. population by the time they are seventy-two years old—require transfusions of blood or blood products. According to the American Blood Commission, each year about 8 million Americans, or 4 percent of our population, donate roughly 12 million units of blood.[1] Thus the organization of our blood-banking system and the quality of blood it collects ultimately affect much of our society.

Blood has been called the "gift of life," but too often it transmits dangerous pathogens. American public health today is lower than necessary because the quality of blood is lower than necessary. Each year 7 to 12 percent of transfusion patients—over 200,000 persons—contract hepatitis, a serious infection of the liver. Roughly a third of this group become ill. Some recover, but others develop chronic liver disease or spread hepatitis to family and friends. Some die.

In 1983 it became clear that blood could transmit a new, incurable, and terrifying disease—the acquired immune deficiency syndrome (AIDS). Over sixty cases were reported through mid-1984. They received substantial media attention, and fear of AIDS led some patients to reject transfusions or postpone elective surgery. Other patients wanted to avoid "potluck" blood from our enormous donor pool by asking friends or family to designate donations for their use. The major nonprofit blood collectors, however, acting in concert, discounted the risks of transfusion-transmitted AIDS, rejected requests for designated donations, and made only slight improvements in their rules for screening high-risk donors.

This situation contains elements of paradox. Posttransfusion hepatitis is common, and new pathogens menace our blood supply even though a decade ago the U.S. government adopted a policy designed to reduce these risks. The Department of Health, Education, and Welfare (HEW) announced the National Blood Policy in 1973, embracing the hypothesis put forth in a book by Richard M. Titmuss, *The Gift Relationship*.[2] Titmuss contended that blood bought by for-profit firms necessarily transmitted more disease than blood donated to nonprofit blood banks. HEW's policy denigrated cash blood and for-profit collectors. It encouraged the regional monopolization or cartelization of nonprofit blood banks in the belief that competition for donors was inefficient.

The National Blood Policy is now the problem rather than the solution. To maintain blood quality, it relies strictly on noncash donors, many of whom give infrequently. This approach yields too many essentially random, walk-in donors who are not screened well enough to minimize the transmission of pathogens that cannot be detected by specific blood tests. Higher-quality blood requires that we use a smaller donor pool of healthy persons who give regularly.

Until recently it has been difficult to know whether the quality of blood could be improved, because many communities have only one organization that collects blood and supplies it to hospitals. A natural test emerged, however, during the AIDS crisis in 1983. Many consumers wanted higher-quality blood than the nonprofit collectors would provide. The competitive, for-profit manufacturers of blood products adopted stricter standards for screening cash plasma suppliers than nonprofit collectors adopted for noncash blood donors. These responses were contrary to what Titmuss's hypothesis would have predicted.

My thesis is that blood quality is now lower than necessary because blood banking is usually monopolized or cartelized. Blood bankers will have stronger incentives to collect the quality of blood that consumers want if the survival of their organizations is at stake—in communities where consumers may choose among nonprofit collectors or for-profit collectors as they now choose physicians and hospitals. A partial remedy would be to adopt a new federal policy encouraging competition by removing the unwarranted stigma that still applies to collecting blood for profit.

Chapter 2 reviews the controversy over the relation between cash blood and posttransfusion hepatitis in the 1960s and early 1970s. It was true that some cash blood collected by for-profit firms was more dangerous than noncash blood, because such firms often bought inexpensive blood from poor and destitute people who did not realize they had been ill. Later it was learned that such persons were high-risk carriers of hepatitis. But some cash blood was not much worse than noncash blood, and some was better. In particular, blood from hospital registries of carefully screened persons who supplied it repeatedly was safer—whether or not they received cash—than noncash blood from largely random, walk-in donors. Experience suggests that the amount and severity of posttransfusion disease would fall if registries were employed by nonprofit and for-profit collectors.

4

Chapters 3 and 4 sketch the history of the American National Red Cross (ANRC), the dominant blood-banking organization in the United States. It was incorporated by Congress late in the nineteenth century as the government's official volunteer relief agency. Its blood program for the armed forces began during World War II and was extended to civilian purposes in 1948. The ANRC moved along several fronts in the ensuing thirty-five years to secure a monopoly in blood banking with as much governmental support to sanction it as possible. This goal was not achieved owing to opposition by other blood collectors. But recognizing the ANRC's goal helps explain some of its interest-group behavior. I argue that economic self-interest is an important motive for nonprofit and for-profit collectors alike.

Chapter 5 analyzes the attempts of blood and plasma collectors to reduce the risks of posttransfusion AIDS. The evidence indicates that for-profit firms are not performing a social disservice by purchasing plasma.

Chapter 6 raises the central question: Is the interest of consumers in better public health advanced by a federal policy that serves the organizational self-interests of nonprofit blood collectors? I suggest ways to improve the quality of blood whether it is sold or donated. I also analyze the likely consequences of alternative institutional arrangements that encourage fewer donors, more quality competition, less monopoly, and strict liability of blood banks for posttransfusion disease.

Notes

1. American Blood Commission, *Fact Sheet: Blood and Its Use* (Arlington, Va., n.d.), p. 1. The American Blood Commission does not collect data on the number of Americans who receive transfusions of blood or blood products each year. The estimate of 3 million is used in U.S. Congress, Congressional Research Service, *AIDS: Acquired Immune Deficiency Syndrome* (Washington, D.C.: Library of Congress, Issue Brief No. IB83162, by Judith A. Johnson, rev. March 27, 1984), p. 10; and Richard D. Aach and Richard A. Kahn, "Post-Transfusion Hepatitis: Current Perspectives," *Annals of Internal Medicine*, vol. 92 (1980), p. 544.

2. Richard M. Titmuss, *The Gift Relationship: From Human Blood to Social Policy* (New York: Vintage Books, 1972).

2

The Controversy over
Cash Blood and
Posttransfusion Hepatitis

Blood transfusion and other forms of blood-based therapy are appropriately regarded as the earliest and presently most highly developed aspect of human tissue transplantation. This policy is directed exclusively to problems of the blood supply, processing and distribution system, and the use of blood. Its basic principles, however, . . . are appropriate to a broader system which must soon be developed to encompass all transplantable human tissues. . . .

. . . The ultimate aims of this policy are improvement in the quality of the supply of blood and blood products and development of an appropriate ethical climate for the increasing use of human tissues for therapeutic medical purposes.

NATIONAL BLOOD POLICY[1]

Hepatitis, a serious and debilitating illness, was common among blood transfusion patients in the 1960s and early 1970s. In 1963 research linked it conclusively to a blood-borne virus, and in 1973 the U.S. government adopted the National Blood Policy to raise the quality of blood by encouraging its donation and discouraging its sale.

The National Blood Policy led to a drastic reorganization of the blood supply industry. In the 1960s blood for direct transfusion was collected by three kinds of organizations. About half was donated to the American National Red Cross (ANRC). About one-quarter was sold to for-profit firms. The remainder was donated to nonprofit local blood banks operated by hospitals, governments, medical societies, or community groups. By the late 1970s commercial blood banks, stigmatized by a hostile federal policy, had virtually withdrawn from this market. Another goal of federal policy was to reduce competition for donors among nonprofit blood banks through regionalization.

Although posttransfusion hepatitis was a major public health problem in the 1970s, the drives against cash blood and competitive blood banking were not effective ways to raise quality. The danger of blood-transmitted hepatitis or acquired immune deficiency syndrome (AIDS) remains unnecessarily great because of our failure to consider or adopt superior policy alternatives.

The National Blood Policy

Richard M. Titmuss, who was professor of social administration at the London School of Economics and Political Science, compared the division between commercial and nonprofit blood collectors in this country during the 1960s with the nationalized system in the United Kingdom.[2] He alleged that the American system not only created more shortages of blood but also wasted more, was administratively inefficient, and cost patients more. These hypotheses were challenged as confusing and unsupported by evidence by American economists of various points of view.[3] But his main thesis—that cash blood necessarily caused higher rates of posttransfusion hepatitis—was not challenged by economists until it had already received widespread support among nonprofit blood collectors and influential physicians.

Titmuss was not writing for economists, whose theory and approach he strongly criticized.[4] Kenneth J. Arrow saw Titmuss as "concerned . . . with the insidious nature of a price system" and having "a passionately informed commitment to an ideal social order."[5] Titmuss argued in 1967 that social services and social administration involved "moral transactions, embodying notions of gift-exchange, of reciprocal obligations," designed and institutionalized to promote social cooperation and community.[6] He thought that society should remove the allocation of blood from the "economic market" involving transactions between strangers to the "social market" involving gifts between strangers. He argued in *The Gift Relationship* in 1971 that permitting donors to designate the recipient of their gift or permitting "the forces of market coercions" to operate would reduce the amount of higher-quality blood given altruistically.[7]

Arrow thought that Titmuss's arguments had "a rather elitist flavor."[8] Robert M. Solow found "a slight, rather typically Fabian, authoritarian streak in Titmuss."[9] The *New York Times* judged his book one of the seven best of 1971. It got the attention of Secretary Elliot Richardson of the Department of Health, Education, and Welfare (HEW). According to J. Garrott Allen, a Stanford University surgeon who opposed cash blood, the book was "of substantial help" in "stimulating [Richardson's] interest in an all-volunteer, uniform national blood program."[10]

7

Congress could not resolve the cash blood controversy with legislation. So it delegated planning authority to HEW and the National Institutes of Health in the National Heart, Blood Vessel, Lung, and Blood Act of 1972.[11] In 1973 HEW announced the National Blood Policy:

> *To encourage, foster, and support efforts designed to bring into being an all-voluntary blood donation system and to eliminate commercialism in the acquisition of whole blood and blood components for transfusion purposes.* The ultimate aims of this policy are improvement in the quality of the supply of blood and blood products and development of an appropriate ethical climate for the increasing use of human tissues for therapeutic medical purposes.[12]

HEW also believed in regionalizing nonprofit blood collectors—promoting consolidation or cooperation rather than competition. It expected this to yield economies of scale in recruiting donors, processing blood, and inventories. (Investigating these hypotheses is beyond the scope of this study.) The policy said:

> If a regional system is not large enough to support adequate recruiting activities, it should merge with another system. A community that is able to meet its blood needs with little promotional effort will receive blood at less expense than a more apathetic community that requires high expenditures for recruiting. . . .
>
> Efforts to recruit volunteer donors must be centrally coordinated in a geographic area and not competitive between systems. Every organization endorsing the goals of the National Blood Policy should use its influence to encourage this concept.[13]

The policy was published in the *Federal Register* but was never supported by legislation or enforced through penalties. It applied only to blood collected for transfusion, not to plasma bought for further manufacture into products for transfusion or laboratory use. Most plasma in the United States is still bought, and U.S. firms dominate the world market for plasma products.

In 1975 the U.S Food and Drug Administration (FDA) wanted to raise the demand for noncash blood by hastening regional conversion to "all-volunteer" donors. It proposed regulations to require that blood and blood components bear (1) a statement distinguishing volunteer (noncash) from paid (cash) blood and (2) a warning that "blood collected from paid donors is associated with a higher risk of transmitting hepatitis than blood from volunteer donors." The ANRC for some time had labeled its blood "volunteer."[14] The U.S. Council on Wage and Price Stability argued that labeling would raise the cost of blood owing both to the extra resources necessary to attract noncash blood and to less competition among blood collectors. The FDA's final regulation included the label but not the warning statement. Economists at the council thought this vindicated their argument that carefully screened cash blood was safe.[15]

To implement its policy, HEW in 1975 created the American Blood Commission (ABC), a loose federation of private sector organizations connected with blood banking. The ABC attempts to coordinate their activities and reduce competition for donors among blood collectors. It is supported by gifts, government grants, and membership dues. Its thirty-seven member organizations in 1984 included associations of medical personnel, hospitals, health insurers, consumers of blood products, medical research charities, the AFL-CIO, the American Legion, the United Way of America, the Veterans Administration, and the three main blood-collecting organizations. These are the American Association of Blood Banks (AABB), 2,300 local blood banks and hospital transfusion services that collect about a third of the nation's blood; the Council of Community Blood Centers, twenty large, independent regional blood banks; and the ANRC.[16] Although the ABC's bylaws do not exclude for-profit members, the American Blood Resources Association—eighty firms making plasma products for transfusion or laboratory use—refused to join after suing unsuccessfully to prevent the National Blood Policy from taking effect.[17]

In its first eight years the ABC promoted the concept of noncash blood, which is intrinsic to its existence and permeates its bylaws and articles of incorporation.[18] It also "concentrated on building a consensus among its membership."[19] The threat of stronger federal action if the ABC failed was supposed to assist this process. Agreement was possible on technical matters but not on key nationwide issues involving the irreconcilable self-interests of the two main nonprofit blood collectors—the ANRC and the AABB. Their conflict, which is described in chapter 4, has been over territory, federal regulations, and the ANRC's goal of monopoly. The ANRC's board of governors first announced in 1972 that "there should be a voluntary, nationwide, nonprofit blood service with uniform standards of operation—medical, technical, and administrative."[20]

The Viral Connection

Hepatitis is such a serious and insidious disease that it warrants an appropriate public health policy today just as much as in the early 1970s. It is, as the name suggests, an inflammation of the liver. It can produce malaise, anorexia, fever, nausea, and jaundice. The only therapy for its acute stage is bed rest and good nutrition. Because hepatitis is usually self-limiting and many attacks are so mild that the victim is unaware of having the disease if it is not confirmed by blood tests, the number of cases diagnosed or reported is understated. But it can lead to chronic liver dysfunction and death. Chronic hepatitis is endemic to Asia and Africa and is associated with cirrhosis and liver cancer, which in some areas of the world is the most common malignancy among males.[21]

Hepatitis is caused by what appear to be at least four extremely successful and insidious viral agents, of which only two have been identified. Hepatitis A used to be called infectious hepatitis because it is transmitted from person to person and by contaminated food and water in areas of poor sanitation. It is the most common type on the planet but not in the United States, where its mortality rate is less than 0.001. Its incubation period is relatively short, and it does not usually become chronic. Hepatitis B used to be called serum hepatitis owing to the discovery in the early 1940s that it was a risk of blood transfusion or drug abuse through unsterilized, multiple-use needles and syringes. Now it is known to be transmitted in more ways than type A, is more insidious and serious (especially for adults), and has mortality rates of about 0.01 in the United States. Of persons with liver cancer, 80 to 90 percent show evidence of hepatitis B, but no causal relation between the two has been established.[22]

It had long been anticipated that hepatitis B's agent was viral. A particle of the virus—called the hepatitis B surface antigen (abbreviated as HBsAg)—was found in 1963 by geneticist Baruch S. Blumberg and his associates of the Institute for Cancer Research in Philadelphia, in a masterpiece of scientific detection for which he received the Nobel Prize in Medicine for 1976.[23] One of Blumberg's crucial findings was that hepatitis B had an asymptomatic carrier state. Not everyone infected by the virus—that is, whose blood is antigen-positive—demonstrates clinical hepatitis B. What makes this virus so insidious is that many persons reach a metabolic "parasite-host" equilibrium with it early in incubation. They become Typhoid Mary carriers in addition to or instead of becoming ill. This condition is estimated to affect 0.1 to 1.0 percent of the population in the United States (about 800,000 persons), 1 to 3 percent in South America, 3 to 6 percent in the Soviet Union and southern Europe, and 10 percent or more in Asia and sub-Saharan Africa—an estimated 200 million carriers. (Hepatitis A can be transmitted during its acute stage but has no known chronic carrier state.)[24]

The blood of hepatitis B carriers is permanently dangerous for transfusion purposes. But carriers can also transmit the virus by intimate contact with family members through mucous membranes or skin cuts, saliva, sneeze droplets, tears, and most bodily excretions. Communal bathing, sharing razors or toothbrushes, and sexual contact are likely paths of transmission. So are such commercial contacts as ear piercing, tattooing, manicures, acupuncture, and dental examinations. The virus can also be communicated from mother to fetus. High-risk populations either as carriers or as victims of hepatitis B include immigrants from high-incidence countries; patients and staffs in mental hospitals; patients receiving multiple blood transfusions; prisoners; users of illicit drugs; homosexually active males; morticians; and patients and staffs in hemodialysis units, dental offices, surgery and emergency rooms, laboratories, and blood banks.[25] Physicians have a risk of contracting hepatitis B that is five to eight times greater than that of the general population. At the Johns Hopkins Medical Institutions in 1984, infectivity rates among medical students increased fourfold after four years and tenfold after six. Some 44 percent of dental personnel were also found to be infected at the time of the study.[26]

Another implication of Blumberg's discovery was that hepatitis B could be partially interdicted by preventing carriers from giving blood. Carriers were more likely to be found among lower socioeconomic groups in high-density areas with poor health and sanitation facilities. Commercial blood banks often were located in skid row areas to be close to downtown hospitals and to inexpensive sources of supply. They bought extensively from poor and destitute people, many of whom may not have known that they had been sick or were carriers. Of those who did, it was assumed that alcoholics and drug addicts would be more willing than other people to give false health histories for a few dollars.

By the late 1970s most observers agreed that the rate of posttransfusion hepatitis had decreased, although it still attacked at least 7 percent of transfusion patients.[27] Many gave the credit to the National Blood Policy, although it could not be established that the decline in cash blood was mainly responsible for the decrease. Other forces were at work simultaneously to reduce hepatitis rates: physicians probably began to transfuse less as they learned more about the risks; laboratory tests for HBsAg improved; and some blood banks moved to shopping centers and college areas.

The assumption that hepatitis B was the only form of posttransfusion hepatitis was shattered in 1975 and 1978 when researchers discovered that HBsAg-negative blood from noncash donors could convey hepatitis. The new strains were neither type A nor type B. Apparently type B had accounted for only about 10 percent of cases all along. Non-A, non-B hepatitis is probably caused by at least two unidentified viruses. It can become chronic and is transmitted like type B but is even more insidious. More than one-third of those infected become carriers, whereas only about 10 percent of those infected with type B do so.[28] Some victims have had up to four distinct bouts of acute hepatitis—circumstantial evidence for two or more non-A, non-B viruses. Antibodies that the patient's immune system produces in response to one type of hepatitis virus usually give protection against additional viruses of that type but not against viruses of other types. Tests for HBsAg do not detect type non-A, non-B hepatitis, and the new vaccine for type B is not effective against it. These extraordinarily successful agents can remain active for a prolonged period in asymptomatic carriers and are resistant to storage, freezing, and dehydration in a vacuum.[29]

The Nature of Payment

The definitions of paid (cash) and volunteer (noncash) in the language of blood collectors are enigmatic to an economist. All blood suppliers or donors have decided freely; even prisoners who have received slightly earlier paroles in exchange for blood could have refused. Most persons who have offered blood have been compensated somehow if not by cash. Before the National Blood Policy, one or more of the following rewards was common: (1) from $5 to $30 according to blood type or other characteristics; (2) theater or athletic tickets, food, wallets, tool kits, and photograph albums; (3) furlough time for soldiers or released time for some workers; (4) credit toward hospital bills; (5) credit toward fees that some hospitals charged when patients used more blood than they replaced; (6) participation in "insurance" plans at certain nonprofit blood centers; and (7) medals or media recognition for repeated donations.[30]

Each reward had an equivalent dollar value, depending on the person's preference for, say, public recognition versus what most of us would consider a small value of cash or gifts. Variations in tastes and regional blood-banking practices in such a large country may explain why so many types of compensation persisted. Titmuss's imprecise survey of blood collected in the United States during the late 1960s indicated that only 9 percent of American donors were altruistic.[31] Moreover, as was argued by Titmuss's chief American critic, Reuben Kessel, it was not clear that noncash blood would be safer. The knowledge of having had hepatitis or the incentive to conceal it might be no greater for someone who wanted to sell blood than for someone who wanted time off from work, a turkey, or credit for a portion of a hospital bill.[32]

The FDA definitions, adopted in 1978, ignored such nuances:

(i) A paid donor is a person who receives monetary payment for a blood donation.

(ii) A volunteer donor is a person who does not receive monetary payment for a blood donation.

(iii) Benefits, such as time off from work, membership in blood assurance programs, and cancellation of nonreplacement fees that are not readily convertible to cash, do not constitute monetary payment.[33]

The FDA retained the "paid-versus-volunteer" terminology because it was commonly used and because "the American Red Cross, which collects only from volunteer donors, identifies its blood as 'volunteer donor' blood." These definitions removed the donor-incentive plans of some nonprofit blood collectors from the paid category.[34] But they also raised ambiguities. In 1979 a Dallas blood bank offered Sears gift certificates to "volunteers." It canceled the program after learning that Sears allowed the certificates' value to be taken mostly in cash.[35]

The use of cash blood varied among countries in the 1970s. Sweden appears to have had low rates of posttransfusion hepatitis with cash blood while Japan had high rates with noncash blood. Since establishing which patients get hepatitis requires careful monitoring and follow-up, disease rates are difficult to document even in developed countries. Apparently Red Cross societies collected enough noncash blood to meet demand in such small countries as Belgium, Finland, Luxembourg, the Netherlands, Norway, and Switzerland. France occasionally relied on placental blood because of too few noncash donors and a prohibition of cash blood. The People's Republic of China offered cash and holidays. Cash was common in India, where in some areas suppliers formed labor unions to negotiate fees. Fees were higher at private blood banks than at government hospitals or the Indian Red Cross. Some patients contracted with individual suppliers. Cash blood has also been employed in Ceylon, Egypt, Iraq, and North Korea.

Cash blood was once predominant in Soviet bloc countries, although by the early 1980s it accounted for less than half. Unpaid "donors" in the Soviet Union recently received meals before and after donating, refunds for lost work time based on the national average wage, extra paid holidays, free recreation and transportation tickets, free medical examinations, and perhaps priority in convalescent homes. These rewards were relatively large, for the quantity of blood drawn on each occasion in the Soviet Union was half that taken in most Western countries.[36]

Lingering Doubts

Titmuss's criticism of cash blood triumphed quickly owing to support from the U.S. government, influential physicians, and nonprofit blood collectors. Apparently less than 10 percent of blood was bought in 1971, and the amount fell to a trickle a few years after the National Blood Policy was adopted. What was unclear about Titmuss's argument was why all cash blood should be denigrated just because some of it was bad. The deficiency of the U.S. blood collection system was not caused by cash blood per se. It was caused by using too much blood from people in poor health.

In the 1960s, before the viral connection was made or became well known, it was rational for commercial blood banks to use the least expensive blood that was believed to be safe. Their services were in demand because they often made quicker deliveries in emergencies to hospitals, offered longer operating hours, and carried larger inventories than the nonprofit blood banks. The for-profit firms also grew because the nonprofit collectors could often not provide enough noncash blood. "Although organized along nonprofit lines, all non–Red Cross blood banks until the 1970's purchased some of their blood, and a few . . . purchased all of it."[37]

Everyone at the time should have realized that whether blood was dangerous was independent of whether it was paid for in cash. Without foolproof blood tests to detect all the various hepatitis viruses, what was important was the location of blood banks and the screening that suppliers were given. Even today, nonprofit blood collectors continue to solicit noncash donations from hospital workers, who give because they know the importance of blood therapy for their patients. But evidence shows that they are high-risk carriers of hepatitis.

The key to safer blood is to screen out high-risk suppliers in all socioeconomic groups. As Kessel argued in attacking Titmuss's position, what was wrong was not that some persons received cash but that healthy persons were not paid enough to provide 100 percent of the desired inventory.[38] Competition among blood banks would have led some of them to establish brand-name reputations for higher-quality blood that patients and physicians would have trusted and patronized. Such competition over quality occurred during the AIDS crisis in 1983, when for-profit manufacturers of plasma products adopted tighter screening standards for cash plasma suppliers than the non-profit collectors adopted for blood donors.

It might also have occurred in the early 1970s if commercial blood banks had been allowed the necessary time to adjust before the National Blood Policy was adopted. It would surely have occurred if blood banks—commercial and nonprofit—had been held strictly liable in tort for posttransfusion hepatitis whether or not they had been negligent in collecting or distributing blood. The quality of blood was difficult to ascertain whether or not it was paid for in cash. But it would have been less costly for blood banks to uncover high-risk characteristics of cash or noncash suppliers than for physicians, hospitals, or patients to attempt to do so. As Kessel argued, holding blood banks rather than patients liable for the consequences of disease would have strengthened their incentives to screen suppliers more carefully.[39]

While cash blood was under attack, both for-profit and nonprofit blood banks won legislation in most states exempting them from strict liability for whole blood and blood products unless negligence could be proved. Most states defined blood and blood products as inherently hazardous materials. Courts interpreted negligence so narrowly that few victims of hepatitis could win damages. The for-profit and especially the nonprofit blood banks, as Kessel explained, sought to escape liability:

> The additional financial incentives of strict liability will mobilize the resources of the market to find and utilize economical supplies of high quality blood. Probably a thoroughgoing system of professional blood donors will develop, professionals being usually better than amateurs. . . . Hence imposing strict liability for blood would eliminate voluntarism and explains the hostility towards commercial blood procurement by voluntary agencies.[40]

Transferring liability from patients to blood banks would also have led the blood banks to buy malpractice insurance or to insure themselves. Passing these costs on to patients might have been more difficult for nonprofit blood banks owing to their opposition to charging for blood.

As with any communicable disease, the way to reduce rates of posttransfusion hepatitis regardless of the rule of liability would be to restrict rather than increase contact with high-risk persons. Registries of "pedigreed" suppliers would require each of the following steps: (1) Take a comprehensive health history and test each supplier's blood regularly for HBsAg and other identifiable agents or abnormalities linked with transfusion diseases. (2) Screen new suppliers for these agents or abnormalities before even the first unit of their

15

blood is transfused. (3) Match hepatitis cases with particular suppliers. (4) Remove suppliers with tainted blood. (5) Use as few suppliers as is consistent with their good health, and add recruits only when essential from groups at low a priori risk. (6) If necessary, pay this smaller group of known, safer suppliers enough to ensure their repeated participation.[41]

The main differences between the registry approach and current nonprofit blood-banking practice are steps 5 and 6. In 1981 about 8 million Americans—a large fraction of whom were random walk-ins—donated whole blood an average of 1.5 times each.[42] Blood collectors realize that healthy persons who donate regularly are more desirable. But without cash incentives, too few will donate the maximum of five times per year that is medically safe. Thus collectors appeal to altruism to get more people to donate less frequently. The alternative is shortages—particularly during summers and holidays—which are undesirable and embarrassing.

Donors and donations to ANRC blood services for the Los Angeles–Orange counties region in 1983 are shown in table 1 by sex and age. Of 440,593 persons in the region's three-year active donor file, only 271,312 or about 62 percent, gave once or more during 1983.[43] Men made almost half again as many donations as women, and the percentage of donors who were men increased with the number of donations while the percentage of women declined.

The disproportionately smaller number of women donors is unfortunate since women are less likely to be carriers of either hepatitis or AIDS. One reason why fewer women donate blood is that some have hemoglobin or body weight below the minimum acceptable levels. Moreover, blood centers may be inconvenient for women who work at home. Collectors may send mobile units to plants and business firms with many employees, especially if donors are compensated with time off work, which also encourages more men. Not much can be done about body weight and hemoglobin levels, but collectors should try to attract more women donors who meet health criteria.

A donor pool like that of the ANRC's Los Angeles–Orange counties region is relatively dangerous to transfusion patients because of its instability. The executive director of ANRC blood services for the region, Carroll L. Spurling, stated in 1984: "All of our donors are asked at each donation if they have previously given blood. Around 25 percent answer that it is their first donation; about 75 percent indicate that they have given blood previously at some time."[44]

He also wrote:

About 75 percent of the blood supply in this area comes from repeat donors whose prior donations are not known to have

TABLE 1

BLOOD DONORS AND DONATIONS TO THE AMERICAN RED CROSS, LOS ANGELES–ORANGE COUNTIES REGION, BY AGE AND SEX, 1983

Number of Donations	Donor Count	Donation Count	Percentage of Total	Percent Male	Percent Female
1	183,808	183,808	45.3	57.4	42.6
2	56,868	113,736	28.0	58.2	41.8
3	19,098	57,294	14.1	59.4	40.6
4	7,517	30,068	7.4	61.0	39.0
5	3,464	17,320	4.3	66.3	33.7
Over 5[a]	557	3,342	0.8	76.1	23.9
Total	271,312	405,568	100.0	58.7	41.3

Number of donors with no donations in 1983: 169,281

Age Group	Donor Count	Donation Count	Percentage of Total	Percent Male	Percent Female	Average No. of Donations
Under 20	35,777	44,342	10.9	54.0	46.0	1.239
20–24	44,415	62,951	15.5	55.9	44.1	1.417
25–29	44,535	66,197	16.3	59.5	40.5	1.486
30–34	35,271	53,553	13.2	58.3	41.7	1.518
35–39	30,351	46,884	11.6	58.4	41.6	1.545
40–44	23,926	36,960	9.1	57.9	42.1	1.545
45–49	18,854	29,958	7.4	61.0	39.0	1.589
50–54	16,430	26,916	6.6	63.9	36.1	1.638
55–59	13,337	22,648	5.6	62.8	37.2	1.698
60–64	7,460	13,369	3.3	66.1	33.9	1.792
65 and over	956	1,790	0.4	66.3	33.7	1.872
Total	271,312	405,568	100.0	58.7	41.3	1.495

NOTE: Percentages may not add to 100.0 because of rounding.
a. Presumably due to inaccurate history, because donors are not supposed to give more than five times in twelve months.
SOURCE: Carroll L. Spurling, executive director, American Red Cross Blood Services, Los Angeles–Orange Counties Region, Los Angeles, June 19, 1984.

caused any problems. Further donations from this large group are solicited repeatedly. However, carefully screened first-time donors have to be added continually in order to provide enough blood for this or any other region.[45]

The issue of how well donors were being screened in 1984 is taken up in chapter 5, but consider for the moment only the stability of the Red Cross donor pool for the Los Angeles area. A statistical technique known as the Markov transition matrix calculates the stability of a group in which a given percentage must be replaced each year. Now make the relatively strong assumption that 75 percent of one year's donors give again the next year and in each of the next four years. This assumption means that the probability of their donating in each successive year is unrelated to the number of previous years in which they have donated. If we begin with a group of people who are all donors, a Markov calculation shows that only 26.2 percent of them are still donating after five years.

In 1976 attitudes of donors were surveyed among 460 households in three U.S. cities by Alvin W. Drake, Stan N. Finkelstein, and Harvey M. Sapolsky. They found that 44 percent of those surveyed had given blood at least once. Sixty-one percent of the men and 30 percent of the women had given. Of the men, 66 percent aged thirty-one to forty and 80 percent aged forty-one to fifty had given. About as many persons had given over ten times (22 percent) as had given once (20 percent).[46] But few students of the problem have acknowledged the dangers to patients of a donor pool of this size and composition— about 8 million persons in the early 1980s (before AIDS), many of whom do not give regularly, and more men than women.

Recently the American Blood Commission claimed that "even though a new strain of [non-A, non-B] hepatitis has been identified for which no screening test has been developed, the risk of posttransfusion hepatitis is minimal today."[47] Presumably the commission believed that the risks were minimal because cash blood was gone.

Whether one could agree with the commission's judgment that the risk of getting posttransfusion hepatitis is minimal in the sense that the risk is *low* depends on one's attitude toward risk. The attack rate for posttransfusion hepatitis of all types from noncash blood in the mid-1970s was about 7 percent.[48] A study of 1,513 transfusion patients between 1974 and 1979 who received an average of 3.7 units of blood— some cash but mainly noncash—was published in the *New England Journal of Medicine* in 1981. The attack rate for non-A, non-B hepatitis was 10 percent.[49] These results were confirmed by a study also published in 1981 in the *Journal of the American Medical Association* in which 283 open-heart surgery patients received an average of 12 units of noncash blood. The attack rate for hepatitis of all kinds was 12.7 percent, 97 percent of which was non-A, non-B.[50] The blood in both studies had been screened for HBsAg.

Assuming that about 3 million patients receive transfusions each year, 210,000 new cases of hepatitis will occur with an attack rate of 7 percent, and 381,000 will occur with a rate of 12.7 percent. Most of this will be relatively insidious type non-A, non-B hepatitis. The probability—between one in fourteen and one in eight—of getting hepatitis from a therapy that is supposed to improve health strikes me as not very favorable odds.

Whether or not one could agree with the American Blood Commission's judgment that the risk of getting hepatitis is minimal in the sense that the risk is *irreducible* depends on the availability of techniques for improved screening of donors. Both studies mentioned above found that non-A, non-B hepatitis was more common in patients who received blood that was high in alanine aminotransferase (ALT), an abnormality that indicates liver disorders. ALT levels can be disclosed by laboratory tests before blood is transfused. One of the studies estimated that discarding 1.6 percent of donated units of blood would eliminate 29 percent of non-A, non-B cases. The other estimated that discarding 3 percent could eliminate about 40 percent of cases. Eliminating this blood could also eliminate about 50 percent of the most severe cases.[51] One study concluded:

> Although ALT screening lacks the sensitivity to detect all infectious units and lacks the specificity to detect only infectious units, the high correlation between an elevated ALT level and infectivity of transfused blood provides a compelling argument that such screening should be instituted. Obviously, if there were sensitive and specific serologic tests for the identification of the non-A, non-B agent or agents, ALT testing would be unnecessary. However, efforts to date to identify such a test have not been rewarding, despite extensive research.[52]

The ALT test was not widely employed in 1984 because blood bankers were worried about the number of safe donors it would reject. The same view applied to using another blood test, the hepatitis core antibody, which appears to be cheaper than the ALT test, and is about equally effective in reducing hepatitis attack rates, but rejects about 6 percent of potential donors.[53] The prospect of cutting non-A, non-B attack rates by perhaps 30 to 40 percent strikes me as promising enough for at least some regions to adopt one test or the other. It is difficult to understand how the risk of hepatitis can be considered irreducible if either test is rarely used.

Waiting for perfect tests for the non-A, non-B agent or agents, rather than implementing surrogate tests in the meantime, subjects more patients to hepatitis risks unnecessarily. It was several years after Blumberg's discovery that the first laboratory test for HBsAg became commercially available, and the hepatitis B vaccine took twenty years. *Waiting for perfect tests for non-A, non-B hepatitis also subjects transfusion patients unnecessarily to new diseases like AIDS.* Since non-A,

19

non-B hepatitis and transfusion-associated AIDS have similar epidemiologies, better screening for the former would almost surely have reduced the incidence of the latter. Apparently about 90 percent of the blood in the high-risk group for AIDS reacts positively to the hepatitis core antibody test.[54] Claims to have isolated the AIDS virus in early 1984 followed a two-year crash program during which over sixty people got AIDS through transfusion. An AIDS vaccine was expected in 1984 to be several years away. The longer blood bankers postpone using additional laboratory tests out of a fear of losing donors, the more AIDS cases will rise.

Why Registries Work

High rates of posttransfusion hepatitis in the 1960s and early 1970s were due in part to scientific ignorance about the several hepatitis viruses and their transmission mechanisms. Some studies before Blumberg's discovery showed that cash blood was implicated in cases of posttransfusion hepatitis as much as six times as frequently as noncash blood.[55] Results of a study published by the National Institutes of Health in 1972 showing that cash blood was about three times as infective are shown in table 2. A study at about the same time showing HBsAg to be more common in cash blood is summarized in table 3.

Blumberg's discovery showed the viral connection, and early blood

TABLE 2

INCIDENCE OF POSTTRANSFUSION HEPATITIS AMONG CARDIOVASCULAR
SURGERY PATIENTS, BY CATEGORY OF DONOR, 1972

Donor Category	Average Number of Units Transfused	Patients Studied	Hepatitis Cases	
			Number	Percent
Volunteer—Red Cross	7.4	715	10	1.4
Volunteer—other	6.4	354	6	1.7
Paid—hospital	6.3	396	13	3.3
Paid—commercial blood bank	4.9	625	33	5.3

NOTE: Study by the National Heart and Lung Institute of patients at fourteen university medical centers.
SOURCE: U.S. General Accounting Office, *Hepatitis from Blood Transfusions: Evaluation of Methods to Reduce the Problem* (Washington, D.C.: Report to the Congress by the Comptroller General, February 13, 1976), p. 7.

TABLE 3
INCIDENCE OF HBSAG AMONG BLOOD DONOR GROUPS, 1972

Donor Category	Number of Donor Groups	Units Tested	Units Positive	Positives per 1,000
Volunteer	21	300,860	506	1.7
Paid	18	117,693	575	4.9
Total	39	418,553	1,081	2.6

NOTE: Survey of thirty-two blood banks in Baltimore, Chicago, Los Angeles, and the National Institutes of Health, using first-generation tests.
SOURCE: General Accounting Office, *Hepatitis from Blood Transfusions*, p. 15.

tests for HBsAg were available a few years later. It was understood when the National Blood Policy was being developed that these early tests were relatively crude. It should have been clear to HEW then that careful donor screening would raise blood quality, especially for non-A, non-B hepatitis, which laboratory tests could not detect. HEW maintained, however, that cash blood was the only culprit.

Evidence available in the mid-1970s showed that registries could reduce transfusion risks whether or not blood was bought. The location of blood banks and the care with which suppliers were screened were what mattered. In developing the basic argument for registries in his 1974 paper, Kessel knew that blood bought by the Mayo clinic was low in hepatitis B carriers. He used this information to show that cash blood was not necessarily inferior to noncash blood. But later evidence showed that the case for registries was stronger than Kessel may have realized.

The Mayo clinic's blood during 1966–1970 was drawn from a registry of 6,000 to 7,000 persons who lived within fifty miles of the clinic, responded to calls within twenty-four hours, and sold or donated an average of about three units per year. About 60 percent received cash. Some suppliers were members of churches that got the cash while the members escaped income taxes.[56] Random walk-in donors who would be accepted at ANRC regional blood centers and other blood banks were not accepted. Table 4 shows the Mayo clinic's claim in 1976 that the combined hepatitis B carrier rates of its cash and noncash donors averaged 0.09 per 1,000 donors between 1969 and 1975. *This was only about one-eighth as much as the blood drawn in the ANRC's north-central region, in which the Mayo clinic is located, the highest-quality Red Cross blood in the United States at the time.* Table 5 shows the Mayo clinic's claim that the incidence among its patients of posttransfusion hepatitis of all types was the lowest of thirteen

TABLE 4

INCIDENCE OF HBSAG AMONG BLOOD DONORS, MAYO CLINIC,
1969–1975, AND AMERICAN RED CROSS, APRIL–DECEMBER 1971

Location	HBsAg-positive Donors (per 1,000)
Mayo Clinic (Rochester, Minnesota)	0.09
American Red Cross regions:	
North-central	0.71
Northwest	0.83
Northeast	1.06
South-central	1.36
Southwest	1.55
Southeast	1.84
Puerto Rico	3.44

SOURCE: Howard F. Taswell, director, Mayo Clinic blood bank, in HEW, *Definitions of Voluntary and Paid Blood Donors* (Bethesda, Md.: National Institutes of Health Main Campus, March 18, 1976, p. 93a); and General Accounting Office, *Hepatitis from Blood Transfusions*, p. 8.

university medical centers. It was approximately to one-fifth that of the lowest group of medical centers (such as Boston, Houston, Indianapolis, and San Francisco) and one-twentieth that of the highest group (Chicago and Los Angeles). The Mayo clinic opposed the FDA labeling and warning regulations because they would falsely stigmatize safe cash blood.[57]

The Massachusetts General Hospital in Boston also excluded walk-ins in 1970–1975. Mobile units were sent to collect blood, and all hepatitis cases were traced. A study of cash versus noncash registries with about equal numbers in each group showed about equal rates of HBsAg carriers. In 1976 the Massachusetts General Hospital opposed the FDA's proposed blood-labeling regulations for the same reasons the Mayo clinic gave.[58]

A 1976 report to the Congress by the U.S. comptroller general compared the qualities of cash and noncash blood in a group of fourteen medical centers. It was the most comprehensive published study of its kind that I found (see table 6). The medical center in Houston that used 100 percent commercial blood ranked sixth of the fourteen. It had a lower rate of posttransfusion hepatitis than one of three hospitals that used less than 1 percent cash commercial blood and two of the four hospitals that used 100 percent noncash blood. The Mayo clinic's blood was the second highest in quality.

TABLE 5

INCIDENCE OF POSTTRANSFUSION HEPATITIS AMONG MEDICAL CENTER
PATIENTS, EARLY 1970s

Location	Incidence of Post-transfusion Hepatitis (per 100 patients)
Rochester, Minnesota	0.4
Minneapolis, Minnesota	0.6
Atlanta, Georgia	2.0
San Francisco, California	2.1
Baltimore, Maryland	2.1
Houston, Texas	2.2
Boston, Massachusetts	2.3
Indianapolis, Indiana	2.6
Columbus, Ohio	3.1
Cleveland, Ohio	3.3
Denver, Colorado	4.5
Chicago, Illinois	8.4
Los Angeles, California	8.6

NOTE: Study by the National Institutes of Health of thirteen major national medical centers.
SOURCE: Howard F. Taswell, director, Mayo Clinic blood bank, in HEW, *Definitions*, p. 91a.

The study reported rates of hepatitis B carriers in 1972 among thirty-nine blood donor groups (table 7). These included twenty-one noncash and eighteen cash groups at thirty-two blood banks in Baltimore, Chicago, Los Angeles, and the National Institutes of Health in Bethesda. It concluded that

> the overall HBsAg positive rate for paid blood was about three times higher than for volunteer blood. A breakdown of the 39 individual donor groups shows, however, that (1) some paid groups had a lower HBsAg positive rate than some volunteer groups and (2) paid blood collected by hospital blood banks had a lower overall positive rate than paid blood collected by commercial blood banks.[59]

The report also found that "of the eight donor groups with positive rates of less than 1 per 1,000, three are paid groups. Each area . . . has some paid donor groups with a lower HBsAg rate than some volunteer donor groups."[60] Entries U and FF in table 7 were cash and noncash groups at one blood bank before and after imposition of the National Blood Policy. The cash group, which was based on regular

23

TABLE 6

INCIDENCE OF POSTTRANSFUSION HEPATITIS AMONG CARDIOVASCULAR
SURGERY PATIENTS, BY PERCENTAGE OF CASH COMMERCIAL BLOOD,
1972

Location	Number of Posttransfusion Hepatitis Cases per 100 Patients	Percentage of Paid Commercial Blood
Lexington, Kentucky	0	3
Rochester, Minnesota	0.5	less than 1
Minneapolis, Minnesota	0.6	less than 1
Atlanta, Georgia	2.0	0
San Francisco, California	2.1	0
Houston, Texas	2.2	100
Baltimore, Maryland	2.3	24
Boston, Massachusetts	2.3	0
Indianapolis, Indiana	2.6	36
Columbus, Ohio	3.1	0
Cleveland, Ohio	3.3	44
Denver, Colorado	4.7	less than 1
Chicago, Illinois	8.1	38
Los Angeles, California	8.6	57
Average	2.8	21

NOTE: Study by the National Heart and Lung Institute of patients at fourteen university medical centers.
SOURCE: General Accounting Office, *Hepatitis from Blood Transfusions*, p. 7.

suppliers, had less than half the HBsAg rate of the noncash group.

The comptroller general found that socioeconomic factors explained 63 percent of the differences among the blood banks' HBsAg rates. The classification of donors as paid or volunteer explained only 36 percent. Both factors were statistically significant but strongly intercorrelated. The report also polled over 1,300 drug addicts in five large cities. It found that about the same percentage donated blood as sold it and that roughly the same split applied to drug addicts after they had had hepatitis.[61]

The report concluded that

certain paid donors—particularly some of those associated with hospital blood banks which obtain blood from well defined and controlled donor populations—are less likely to transmit hepatitis than certain volunteer donors. Eliminating all blood from paid donors should reduce the overall incidence of post-transfusion hepatitis but also

TABLE 7

INCIDENCE OF HBsAg AMONG BLOOD DONOR GROUPS, BY PAID OR
VOLUNTEER STATUS, 1972

Donor Group	Paid or Volunteer	Rate per 1,000	Donor Group	Paid or Volunteer	Rate per 1,000
A	V	0	U	P	2.1
B	V	0	V	P	2.2
C[a]	P	0	W	V	2.8
D	V	0.6	X	V	2.9
E	V	0.8	Y	P	3.0
F	P	0.8	Z	P	3.5
G	P	0.8	AA	V	3.8
H	V	0.9	BB	V	4.1
I	V	1.0	CC	P	4.3
J	P	1.3	DD	P	4.4
K	V	1.3	EE	P	4.4
L	V	1.3	FF	V	4.7
M	V	1.3	GG	P	4.8
N	P	1.4	HH	P	5.0
O	V	1.4	II	V	5.6
P	V	1.5	JJ	P	6.7
Q	V	1.5	KK	P	6.8
R	V	1.8	LL	P	9.0
S	V	1.8	MM	P	11.0
T	V	2.0			

NOTE: Survey of thirty-nine donor groups at thirty-two blood banks in Baltimore, Chicago, Los Angeles, and the National Institutes of Health, using first-generation tests.

a. This blood bank, a National Institutes of Health clinical center, was classified as using cash blood because its donors received $25 for every second unit. About 92 percent of its 1972 donors received cash.

Source: General Accounting Office, *Hepatitis from Blood Transfusions*, p. 15.

—will eliminate a significant amount of paid blood that, in certain cases, is safer than volunteer blood,
—will have no effect on high-risk volunteer blood, and
—could cause blood shortage problems.[62]

It recommended "that the Secretary of HEW promote the establishment of a registry listing individuals unacceptable as blood donors and employ procedures to develop an effective registry system." This federal registry would have been based on hepatitis-antigen sensitivity in blood specimens plus careful records of whose blood was transfused to whom. The purpose was "to help purge the system of high-risk donors—volunteer as well as paid."[63] HEW rejected the idea because it would lead to expenditure of great amounts of money for no certain benefit, on the basis of a concept (maximum acceptable limit for diseases which are conceivably preventable) which is itself unacceptable to a Department charged with responsibility for preventing preventable diseases. In addition, it would place HEW in the untenable position of spending vast sums primarily to assure access to a generally undesirable class of blood donors, and it would do these things to the detriment of an all-voluntary system which would assuredly provide the largest attainable improvement in this situation.[64]

Additional evidence bearing on the cash blood controversy is the conversion during 1972–1974 of the regional monopoly in New Mexico to noncash blood. The incidence of HBsAg did not change significantly.[65] Fitzsimmons Army Medical Center in Denver converted from a stable cash population of active-duty and retired military personnel in 1973 to a noncash population of active-duty personnel in 1974 who received three-day passes for each donation. The rate of HBsAg rose from 0.1 percent to 0.94 percent, but the composition of the pool changed for other reasons.[66]

Medical research has compared hemophiliacs in one city who were treated over one hundred times with clotting materials, each unit of which was prepared from the noncash blood of single donors, with those in another city who were treated with commercial clotting materials prepared from the pooled cash blood of thousands of persons. If cash blood were more dangerous, one would expect higher rates of both HBsAg carriers and hepatitis B disease among the second group of patients. Studies during the mid-1970s, however, disclosed about the same rates for both groups of patients. (Neither group of products was prepared from blood collected through registries.) A similar result was found in Denmark.[67]

Research by a pharmaceutical firm disclosed that the incidence of HBsAg in plasma it purchased to manufacture clotting-factor concentrates during 1974–1976 was between 1.2 and 1.4 per 1,000 persons. The rate of HBsAg in noncash donors during the same era using the same testing methods was 1.25 per 1,000.[68] Neither group was involved in registries.

Conclusions

Evidence from the era when both cash and noncash blood were in use shows that cash blood is not of lower quality if registries are employed and suppliers are screened with sufficient care. One region that converted from a cash system without registries to a noncash system without registries did not change the incidence of hepatitis carriers. I would have expected blood quality to be affected by registries rather than cash payment, so this result is not surprising. Other evidence from this era indicates that blood banks that employed registries had higher-quality blood. Other independent analysts reached similar conclusions.[69]

Registries, like the ALT and hepatitis core antibody tests, err on the safe side by rejecting borderline donors. I could find neither logic nor evidence for the proposition that nonprofit, noncash registries will yield blood of higher quality than for-profit, cash registries, *ceteris paribus*. I could also find neither logic nor evidence to support the proposition that monopolized or cartelized nonprofit blood banks will yield blood of higher quality than competitive, for-profit blood banks—provided that both employ registries. I argue later that both logic and evidence support the proposition that competition among blood banks would improve the quality of blood.

The National Blood Policy took the wrong turn in 1973 by pushing for noncash donors and noncompetitive blood banking rather than for registries and strict liability in tort. It was almost as if the policy makers were more concerned about establishing "an appropriate ethical climate" than about improving public health. Certainly Titmuss was deeply concerned about "social policy" that made "a moral and political decision for society as a whole."[70] These views dominated policy making and contributed to unnecessarily high rates of insidious diseases.

The effect of registries on blood quality is already known. Cash and noncash registries should be experimented with again to learn whether enough high-quality blood can be obtained without paying cash. Many people remain opposed on ideological grounds to buying blood. Some of them may have been influenced by Titmuss's confusion between cash blood per se and low-quality blood as well as by the efforts of American blood collectors to link the two. But they are not linked in analysis or in fact if registries are used, and they should not be linked in policy. The quality of blood depends on the selectivity of the buyers, the nature of the sellers, and the incentives that each group is given—whether or not sellers receive cash. Paying cash may not be necessary to obtain enough high-quality blood in some communities, but in others it may. Being pragmatic about the difference will help to reduce morbidity and mortality.

Notes

1. U.S. Department of Health, Education, and Welfare (HEW), Office of the Secretary, "National Blood Policy: Proposed Implementation Plan; Requests for Comments," *Federal Register*, vol. 39 (1974), p. 9329.

2. Richard M. Titmuss, *The Gift Relationship: From Human Blood to Social Policy* (New York: Vintage Books, 1972).

3. Armen A. Alchian et al., *The Economics of Charity: Essays on the Comparative Economics and Ethics of Giving and Selling, with Applications to Blood* (London: Institute of Economic Affairs, 1973), pp. 107–91; and Kenneth J. Arrow, "Gifts and Exchanges," *Philosophy and Public Affairs*, vol. 1 (1972), pp. 343–62.

4. Economists "often give the impression of possessively owning a hot line to God" (Titmuss, *The Gift Relationship*, p. 199). He believed that the "blinkered" application of "economic arithmetic" to social transactions would "endanger society's unmethodical knowledge of the living man" (ibid., p. 217).

5. Arrow, "Gifts and Exchanges," pp. 360, 362.

6. Richard M. Titmuss, "The Subject of Social Administration," in Titmuss, *Commitment to Welfare* (London: George Allen and Unwin, 1968), pp. 20–22.

7. Titmuss, *The Gift Relationship*, p. 242.

8. Arrow, "Gifts and Exchanges," p. 360.

9. Robert M. Solow, "Blood and Thunder," *Yale Law Journal*, vol. 80 (1971), p. 1711.

10. J. Garrott Allen, "What Price Blood?" *Stanford MD*, Fall 1976, p. 5.

11. National Heart, Blood Vessel, Lung, and Blood Act of 1972, *Statutes at Large*, vol. 86 (1972), pp. 679–87; David B. Johnson, "Introduction: The Blood Market," in David B. Johnson, ed., *Blood Policy: Issues and Alternatives* (Washington, D.C.: American Enterprise Institute, 1977), p. 4; and Rachael Westbrook, James Warner Bjorkman, and Jerry Rose, *The Nonreplacement Fee Controversy and National Blood Policy* (Boston: Intercollegiate Case Clearing House, Case No. 9-379-713, 1979), pp. 36–37.

12. American Blood Commission, *Chronology of the National Blood Policy* (Arlington, Va., n.d.), p. 2; and HEW, "National Blood Policy: Proposed Implementation Plan," pp. 9329–30.

13. HEW, "National Blood Policy: Proposed Implementation Plan," p. 9329.

14. U.S. Food and Drug Administration, "Whole Blood and Red Blood Cells: Label Statement to Distinguish Volunteer from Paid Blood Donors," *Federal Register*, vol. 40 (1975), pp. 53040–43; and idem, "Current Good Manufacturing Practices for Blood and Blood Components; Additional Standards for Human Blood and Blood Products; Whole Blood and Components of Whole Blood Intended for Transfusion; Donor Classification Labelling Requirements; Final Rule," *Federal Register*, vol. 43 (1978), pp. 2142, 2147.

15. James C. Miller III, *Evidence Relevant to CWPS Position on Eliminating Paid Blood* (Washington, D.C.: Executive Office of the President, Council on Wage and Price Stability, September 17, 1976); and Dianne R. Levine, "Labeling Donated Blood," in James C. Miller III and Bruce Yandle, eds., *Benefit-Cost Analysis of Social Regulation: Case Studies from the Council on Wage and Price Stability* (Washington, D.C.: American Enterprise Institute, 1979), pp. 13–19.

16. HEW, Office of the Secretary, "National Blood Policy: Department Responses to Private Sector Implementation Plan," *Federal Register*, vol. 39 (1974), pp. 32702–9; Alvin W. Drake, Stan N. Finkelstein, and Harvey M. Sapolsky, *The American Blood Supply* (Cambridge, Mass., and London: MIT Press, 1982), p. 56; American Blood Commission, "Member Organizations," *ABC News Summary*, annual ed. (Arlington, Va., Fall 1983); and Westbrook et al., *Nonreplacement Fee Controversy*, pp. 87–89.

17. Louanne Kennedy, "Community Blood Banking in the United States from 1937–1975: Organizational Formation, Transformation, and Reform in a Climate of Competing Ideologies" (Ph.D. dissertation, New York University, 1978), pp. 126–27.

18. American Blood Commission, "Articles of Incorporation" (Washington, D.C., March 21, 1975, mimeographed); idem, "Bylaws" (Arlington, Va., April 5, 1975, amended through March 21, 1984); and idem, *ABC News Summary*, Fall 1983.

19. Kennedy, "Community Blood Banking," pp. 423–24; American Blood Com-

mission, *Review of American Blood Commission's Progress and Achievements* (Arlington, Va., n.d.), p. 1; and idem, *Profile of Blood Service Today* (Arlington, Va., n.d.), pp. 2–4.

20. American National Red Cross, Board of Governors, "Essential Features of a National Blood Service" (1972), reprinted in U.S. Public Health Service, National Heart and Lung Institute, National Blood Resource Program, *Summary Report: NHLI's Blood Resource Studies* (Bethesda, Md.: DHEW Publication no. [NIH] 73-416, 1972), pp. 55–56, 65–67.

21. U.S. Public Health Service, Centers for Disease Control, "Inactivated Hepatitis B Virus Vaccine," *Morbidity and Mortality Weekly Report*, vol. 31 (1982), pp. 317–22, 327–28; Richard D. Aach and Richard A. Kahn, "Post-Transfusion Hepatitis: Current Perspectives," *Annals of Internal Medicine*, vol. 92 (1980), pp. 539–46; M. J. P. Arthur et al., "Hepatitis B, Hepatocellular Carcinoma, and Strategies for Prevention," *Lancet* (1984-i), pp. 607–10; Jules L. Dienstag, "Toward the Control of Hepatitis B," *New England Journal of Medicine*, vol. 303 (1980), pp. 874–76; and Robert H. Purcell, "The Viral Hepatitides," *Hospital Practice*, July 1978, pp. 51–63.

22. Purcell, "Viral Hepatitides," p. 63.

23. Baruch S. Blumberg, "Australia Antigen and the Biology of Hepatitis B," *Science*, vol. 197 (1977), pp. 17–25; and James S. Reed and James L. Boyer, "Viral Hepatitis: Epidemiologic, Serologic, and Clinical Manifestations," *Disease a Month*, January 1979, p. 8.

24. Wolf Szmuness et al., "Hepatitis B Vaccine: Demonstration of Efficacy in a Controlled Clinical Trial in a High-Risk Population in the United States," *New England Journal of Medicine*, vol. 303 (1980), pp. 833–41; and Purcell, "Viral Hepatitides," p. 59.

25. Reed and Boyer, "Viral Hepatitis," pp. 13–14; and Public Health Service, Centers for Disease Control, "Inactivated Hepatitis B Virus Vaccine."

26. Sidney D. Kreider and W. Robert Lange, "Hepatitis B Vaccine," *New England Journal of Medicine*, vol. 310 (1984), p. 466.

27. Aach and Kahn, "Post-Transfusion Hepatitis," pp. 539–42; and Harvey J. Alter et al., "Posttransfusion Hepatitis after Exclusion of Commercial and Hepatitis-B Antigen-positive Donors," *Annals of Internal Medicine*, vol. 77 (1972), pp. 691–99.

28. Aach and Kahn, "Post-Transfusion Hepatitis," pp. 539–40, 544; R. K. Haugen, "Hepatitis after the Transfusion of Frozen Red Cells and Washed Red Cells," *New England Journal of Medicine*, vol. 301 (1979), pp. 393–95; Purcell, "Viral Hepatitides," p. 62; Reed and Boyer, "Viral Hepatitis," p. 15; Leonard B. Seeff et al. "VA Cooperative Study of Post-transfusion Hepatitis, 1969–1974: Incidence and Characteristics of Hepatitis and Responsible Risk Factors," *American Journal of the Medical Sciences*, vol. 270 (1975), pp. 355–62.

29. James W. Mosley et al., "Multiple Hepatitis Viruses in Multiple Attacks of Acute Viral Hepatitis," *New England Journal of Medicine*, vol. 296 (1977), pp. 75–78; and E. Tabor and R. J. Gerety, "Non-A, Non-B Hepatitis: New Findings and Prospects for Prevention," *Transfusion*, vol. 19 (November–December 1979), reprinted in *Plasma Quarterly*, vol. 2 (June 1980), pp. 38–39, 52–55.

30. U.S. Public Health Service, National Heart and Lung Institute, National Blood Resource Program, *NHLI's Blood Resource Studies* (3 vols.), vol. 1: *Supply and Use of the Nation's Blood Resource* (Bethesda, Md.: DHEW Publication no. (NIH) 73-417, 1972), pp. 197–200; and Michael H. Cooper and Anthony J. Culyer, *The Price of Blood*, Hobart Paper 41 (London: Institute of Economic Affairs, 1968), p. 42.

31. Titmuss, *The Gift Relationship*, p. 94.

32. Reuben A. Kessel, "Transfused Blood, Serum Hepatitis, and the Coase Theorem," *Journal of Law and Economics*, vol. 17 (1974), p. 289.

33. U.S. Food and Drug Administration, "Current Good Manufacturing Practices, Blood and Blood Products," p. 2147.

34. Ibid., p. 2143; and Public Health Service, National Blood Resource Program, *Supply and Use of the Nation's Blood Resource*, p. 199.

35. American Association of Blood Banks, *News Briefs*, January 12, 1979, p. 5.

36. "Blood Bankers Tour China," *AABB News Briefs*, July 1983, p. 12; Piet J. Hagen, *Blood: Gift or Merchandise* (New York: Alan R. Liss, 1982), pp. 157, 180–83; Lorry Rose, "Super Recruiting in Russia," *American Association of Blood Banks Review*, vol. 2 (Winter 1979), pp. 11–13; Titmuss, *The Gift Relationship*, p. 177; Cooper and Culyer, *The Price of Blood*, p. 26; and Leo Zuckerman, "International Sourcing of Plasma for Diagnostic Products," in W. L. Warner, ed., *Plasma Forum III* (American Blood Resources Association, 1980), pp. 24–25.

37. Kennedy, "Community Blood Banking," p. 115; and Marc A. Franklin, "Tort Liability for Hepatitis: An Analysis and a Proposal," *Stanford Law Review*, vol. 24 (1972), pp. 449–51.

38. Kessel, "Transfused Blood," pp. 287–88.

39. Ibid., pp. 279–82.

40. Reuben A Kessel, "Transfused Blood, Serum Hepatitis, and the Coase Theorem," *Journal of Law and Economics*, vol. 17 (1974), p. 286. Copyright 1974, The University of Chicago. Excerpted by permission of The University of Chicago Press.

41. Ibid., pp. 272–75.

42. Drake et al., *American Blood Supply*, p. 5.

43. Carroll L. Spurling, executive director, American Red Cross Blood Services, Los Angeles–Orange Counties Region, to Ross D. Eckert, Claremont, July 9, 1984, personal files of Ross D. Eckert, Claremont, California.

44. Ibid.

45. Carroll L. Spurling, "Letters to the Times: 'The Threat to Our Blood Supply,'" *Los Angeles Times*, April 27, 1984; and idem, "The Safety of Our Blood Supply: Understanding of Blood Banking Can Mitigate Concerns about AIDS" (Los Angeles, n.d., mimeographed), pp. 1–2.

46. Drake et al., *American Blood Supply*, pp. 76–113, esp. pp. 87–89.

47. American Blood Commission, *Fact Sheet: Blood and Its Use* (Arlington, Va. n.d.), p. 2.

48. Aach and Kahn, "Post-Transfusion Hepatitis," pp. 542, 544.

49. Richard D. Aach et al., "Serum Alanine Aminotransferase of Donors in Relation to the Risk of Non-A, Non-B Hepatitis in Recipients: The Transfusion-Transmitted Viruses Study," *New England Journal of Medicine*, vol. 304 (1981), pp. 989–94.

50. Harvey J. Alter et al., "Donor Transaminase and Recipient Hepatitis: Impact on Blood Transfusion Services," *Journal of the American Medical Association*, vol. 246 (1981), pp. 630–34.

51. Ibid., p. 630; Aach et al., "Serum Alanine Aminotransferase," p. 993; and U.S. Food and Drug Administration, Office of Biologics, *Blood Products Advisory Committee*, vol. 1: *Open Session*, transcript of proceedings (Bethesda, Md., 1983), pp. 160–63.

52. Aach et al., "Serum Alanine Aminotransferase," excerpted by permission of the *New England Journal of Medicine*, vol. 304 (1981), p. 993.

53. "Blood Bank Will Use Second Test in Drive to Reduce AIDS Risk," *Wall Street Journal*, March 30, 1984; Marilyn Chase, " 'Gift of Life' May Be Also an Agent of Death in Some AIDS Cases," *Wall Street Journal*, March 12, 1984; and U.S. Food and Drug Administration, *Blood Products Advisory Committee*, pp. 175, 178.

54. "Blood Bank Will Use Second Test."

55. Aach and Kahn, "Post-Transfusion Hepatitis," p. 542.

56. U.S. General Accounting Office, *Hepatitis from Blood Transfusions: Evaluation of Methods to Reduce the Problem* (Washington, D.C.: Report to the Congress by the Comptroller General, February 13, 1976), p. 8; and Kessel, "Transfused Blood," p. 287.

57. Statements of Christopher O. Batchelder, administrator, and Howard F. Taswell, blood bank director, Mayo Clinic, Rochester, Minnesota, in HEW, *Definitions of Voluntary and Paid Blood Donors* (Bethesda, Md.: National Institutes of Health Main Campus, 1976), pp. 85–90, 91–105.

58. Statement of Charles Huggins, Massachusetts General Hospital, Boston, Massachusetts, in HEW, *Definitions,* pp. 122–24, 127.

59. General Accounting Office, *Hepatitis from Blood Transfusions,* p. 14.

60. Ibid., p. 15.

61. Ibid., pp. 18–23.

62. Ibid., p. i.

63. Ibid., pp. i, ii.

64. Ibid., p. 66.

65. D. MacN. Surgenor and J. F. Cerveny, "A Study of the Conversion from Paid to Altruistic Blood Donors in New Mexico," *Transfusion,* vol. 18 (1978), pp. 54–63.

66. Paul W. Holley et al., "Do Volunteer Donors Decrease Posttransfusion Hepatitis?" *Journal of the American Medical Association,* vol. 234 (1975), pp. 1051–52; and statement of J. Garrott Allen in HEW, *Definitions,* p. 84.

67. Richard B. Counts, "Serum Transaminase and HBsAg Antibody in Hemophiliacs Treated Exclusively with Cryoprecipitate," in Joseph C. Fratantoni and David L. Aronson, eds., *Unsolved Therapeutic Problems in Hemophilia,* Proceedings of a Conference Sponsored by Bureau of Biologics, FDA; Division of Blood Diseases and Resources, NHLBI; and National Hemophilia Foundation (Bethesda, Md.: Public Health Service, National Institutes of Health, DHEW Publication no. (NIH) 77-1089, 1976), pp. 77–79; Carol K. Kasper, "Evaluation of Adverse Reactions in Hemophiliacs from Long Term Exposure to Blood and Blood Products; Abstract of Final Report," U.S. Food and Drug Administration, Contract No. 223-74-1189, June 28, 1976; and Vibeke Holsteen et al., "Hepatitis, Type B in Haemophiliacs: Relation to the Source of Clotting Factor Concentrates," *Scandinavian Journal of Haematology,* vol. 18 (1977), pp. 214–18.

68. Clyde McCaully and K. Knoll, "HBsAg Testing in Commercial Plasmapheresis," *Plasma Quarterly,* vol. 1 (June 1979), pp. 36–37, 62–63; R. Y. Dodd et al., "Hepatitis B (Surface) Antigen Testing by Radioimmunoassay: Experience in a Very Large Volunteer Donor Population," *American Journal of Clinical Pathology,* vol. 63 (1975), pp. 847–53.

69. Drake et al., *American Blood Supply,* pp. 33–38.

70. Titmuss, *The Gift Relationship,* p. 242.

31

3

The American National
Red Cross: Statutory Framework
and Early History

*There is no higher calling or accomplishment than that of bringing
to another person, without expectation of debt, gratitude, or reward,
the kind of help and encouragement that enables one to overcome
an emergency or problem and emerge strengthened, more self-re-
liant.*

JEROME H. HOLLAND, Chairman, and
GEORGE M. ELSEY, President
American National Red Cross[1]

On February 27, 1981, President Ronald Reagan declared March Red
Cross Month and asked Americans to celebrate the centennial of the
American National Red Cross (ANRC) by making voluntary contributions.[2] This was a tribute to the longevity of America's official
voluntary relief agency and to its independence from government
financing.[3] But it was also a reminder of the intimate legal and political
relations between this "quasi-official arm of Government"[4] and the
government itself (and U.S. presidents in particular). Understanding
the processes by which the Red Cross was created and grew is helpful
in understanding its current programs and the policies that it favors.

Genesis and Purposes

War is less horrible, at least in one dimension, in the twentieth century
than it was in the nineteenth when armies, after a battle, usually
moved on after giving minimal aid to their wounded. The superb
work of Florence Nightingale during the Crimean War demonstrated
that many of the wounded could survive with basic sanitary assistance. The 40,000 casualties of the Battle of Solferino in the Austro-

Italian War of 1859 were witnessed by Jean Henri Dunant, a Swiss banker who memorialized the catastrophe in a book acclaimed throughout Europe.[5] Dunant and others organized an international conference, proposing that individual countries establish their own relief committees for battlefield aid plus a permanent, international, voluntary civilian organization. This body would be politically neutral and identifiable in combat zones by its own distinctive flag. These principles were embodied in the Geneva Convention of 1864 and in the creation of the International Committee of the Red Cross.[6] The United States did not sign the Geneva Convention until 1882.

The American Association of the Red Cross was founded in 1881 by Clara Barton, who won national fame for her nursing on Civil War battlefields.[7] It was first incorporated in 1881 in the District of Columbia and reincorporated by an act of Congress in 1900 as the American National Red Cross.[8] Power was vested in Barton and fifty-five social philanthropists. An early feud between factions led by Barton and by Mabel T. Boardman was settled only when President Theodore Roosevelt supported the Boardman group.[9] His support led to Barton's retirement and set a precedent for presidential involvement. A second statutory reincorporation in 1905 gave the president of the United States a larger and permanent role in ANRC affairs.[10]

This statute, as amended in 1947, created a board of fifty governors.[11] The president appoints eight governors, seven of whom must be chosen from agencies or cabinet departments related to Red Cross activities. At least one but not more than three of the seven must be from the armed services. In 1983 these seven officials were the secretaries of state, defense, and education, the secretary and assistant secretary for health of the Department of Health and Human Services (which regulates certain activities of the ANRC's blood program through the Food and Drug Administration), the chairman of the Joint Chiefs of Staff, and the director of the Federal Energy Management Agency. The eighth presidential appointee is the principal officer of the corporation. Thirty governors are elected by local chapters in convention. These thirty-eight governors elect twelve members at large. The eight presidential appointees serve terms that coincide with their federal offices. All other governors serve staggered three-year terms.

In 1983 the honorary chairman of the ANRC was President Reagan, the honorary counselor was the attorney general of the United States, and the honorary treasurer was the secretary of the Treasury. Nowadays the ANRC refers to itself for public relations purposes as the American Red Cross because use of its full statutory name created confusion between the local chapters and the national headquarters in Washington, D.C. Its official name, however, which was widely used until recently and is used throughout this study, is still the American National Red Cross.[12]

The purposes of the ANRC were established by Congress in its original act of incorporation. It has the exclusive right to (1) furnish volunteer aid to the sick and wounded of armies in time of war; (2) perform all duties assigned to national Red Cross societies under the Geneva Convention of 1864 and related U.S. treaty obligations; (3) act in matters of volunteer relief as a medium of communication between the American people and its armed forces; (4) communicate internationally with other Red Cross societies; (5) carry on a system of peacetime national and international relief to mitigate suffering caused by natural disasters; and (6) use the Red Cross name, emblem, and insignia in performing services and soliciting funds or materials (fraudulent use of which by any other person is a misdemeanor punishable by up to one year's imprisonment or a $500 fine payable to the ANRC or both). The ANRC is required by law to submit an annual report of its transactions and finances to the secretary of defense for audit and transmittal to Congress.[13] This requirement established public accountability and an additional measure of governmental control.

The modern ANRC is a large and diverse organization. On June 30, 1983, it had 20,704 career staff, 2,073 of whom were stationed at national headquarters. It had 2,963 local chapters, 1,677 of which were staffed entirely by volunteers. Volunteers providing assistance for disasters, armed services, blood collection, safety, youth activities, international work, public affairs, and chapter governance totaled 1.5 million. Another 5.1 million persons were blood donors, and 2.6 million students participated in programs at elementary and secondary schools. During its fiscal year that ended June 30, 1983, the ANRC collected over $238 million in public support plus revenues of more than $483 million from a variety of activities. Over $418 million came from "cost-recovery" fees collected by ANRC blood services to process, store, handle, and transport blood. Total ANRC expenses exceeded $653 million, of which over $369 million was spent on blood services. Fees and other income to blood services exceeded expenses (after property sales and acquisitions) by almost 8.5 percent, or $36 million.[14]

The ANRC engages in many helpful activities that lie beyond its statutory authority for military and disaster assistance. These include medical research; community services for the handicapped, the elderly, and disadvantaged youth; services and education for public health, first aid, and water safety; the collection and distribution of whole blood for transfusion; and the distribution and sale of products manufactured from blood. Perhaps because of the maternal symbol-

34

ism of its purposes, the importance of nursing to its work, and the decisive roles of women (especially a nurse) in its early leadership, the ANRC since World War I has occasionally been described both internally and in its fund-raising drives as "the Greatest Mother in the World."[15]

Presidential Influence

Foster Rhea Dulles's history of the ANRC's first seventy years, to which the ANRC holds the 1950 copyright, was written under its auspices with the use of its archival material. Dulles described a young and energetic organization that used its official relationship with the U.S. government (as its full name implies), accommodated presidential wishes, protected its exclusive operating rights, and sought to expand and diversify.

Presidents have appointed the ANRC's principal officers since 1905, when Theodore Roosevelt named William Howard Taft. The ANRC could not physically have been much closer to the presidency during the Taft era, when it occupied room 341 of what is now the Old Executive Office Building, adjoining the White House. In 1915 President Woodrow Wilson laid the cornerstone of its permanent headquarters, on government property, on Seventeenth Street, N.W., facing the White House south lawn.[16]

When his term ended in 1913, Taft resigned as principal officer in favor of Wilson. Dulles argued that this established "a new precedent in presidential succession."[17] Wilson established a War Council in 1917. After the war he named his own principal officer, "who was apparently the choice of the outgoing members of the War Council rather than the Old Guard . . ." consisting of Mabel Boardman and other former leaders.[18] Subsequent appointees have been prominent and influential. In 1935 President Franklin D. Roosevelt named Admiral Cary T. Grayson, his "physician and long a close personal friend," and in 1944 chose Basil O'Connor, his former law partner and head of the National Foundation for Infantile Paralysis. President Harry S. Truman named General George C. Marshall in 1949 and E. Roland Harriman in 1950, when Marshall became secretary of defense. President Richard M. Nixon appointed Frank Stanton, former president of the Columbia Broadcasting System. President Jimmy Carter chose Jerome H. Holland, a college president and U.S. ambassador.[19]

Protecting Turf

Clara Barton early saw the value of government protections to her young organization. The primary goal toward which she worked for eighteen years was to obtain a federal charter that would establish

35

her group's legitimacy on a nationwide basis and guarantee its exclusive use of the Red Cross name and insignia.[20] Also during this period she tried, Dulles said, to "forestall any danger of rival societies encroaching on . . . [her] field."[21] A number of local Red Cross groups had been formed under state charters, some of which had as much status and prestige as Barton's group. She discouraged the formation of more local societies until her federal charter was granted, after which they could affiliate.[22]

Barton viewed rival Red Cross societies "with distrust rather than enthusiasm"[23] before incorporation by Congress in 1900. She got President William McKinley to approve her mission to Cuba during the insurrection of 1897 rather than that of a rival.[24] In 1911 President Taft established the ANRC's right to be "the only volunteer society now authorized by this government to render aid to its land and naval forces in time of war." Dulles said that the public announcement of this authorization "had great significance" for the Red Cross, as did legislation a year later authorizing the U.S. Army to provide subsistence for its personnel and to transport its supplies free of charge.[25] These exclusive privileges were jealously guarded but with mixed success owing to growing competition from the American Legion and the Veterans of Foreign Wars.[26] In World War II the ANRC became the only civilian agency permitted to provide medical and social services, clubs, and recreational facilities to expeditionary forces overseas. Earlier the ANRC moved into civil defense but, Dulles says, only after examination and review "with that careful protection of its interests that so often marked Red Cross policy."[27]

During the 1930s the ANRC sought to remain independent of government financing. But this policy ultimately reduced its scope as increasing federalization of social programs eclipsed such traditional ANRC fields as nursing and services to veterans.[28] By the end of the decade it had stronger rivals in the private sector, too. The newer Community Chest organizations sought to participate in the ANRC's very successful fund-raising drives. Dulles recounts the complaint of an ANRC vice-president in a confidential 1941 memorandum that the chests were "busy in an organized way, biting the 'Greatest Mother' in the leg."[29] This dispute was pushed all the way up to President Roosevelt, who maintained the financial independence of the ANRC (then led by his friend and physician, Admiral Grayson).

Taking New Ground

Apparently the ANRC first ventured outside the terms of its statutory authority with a rural public health program in 1907. Dulles said that this "entirely new enterprise" was launched "as a means of providing something for the chapters to do without waiting for a disaster."[30] An internal debate over purposes occurred in 1922. The "strict constructionists" who wanted the organization to remain devoted to war and disaster relief lost to those who wanted it to move in the direction of an amorphous family welfare agency run by social workers. These programs caused border warfare with local charities, public health authorities, and medical societies. Most were scaled back to education and demonstration.[31]

A transfusion service was first proposed by local chapters in 1929. (Blood-banking practices as we know them had yet to be established.) It was initially rejected by the national organization as not being "a proper Red Cross chapter activity." By 1938, however, seven chapters were enrolling donors for hospitals. The ANRC, Dulles said, "moved cautiously in endorsing such blood banks as an authorized national activity, . . . but in April 1939, limited authority was given to the chapters as a whole to develop the program on what was still a highly experimental basis."[32]

Blood transfusions became common early in this century. They were impractical outside hospitals, however, because of the necessary laboratory testing to ensure compatibility between the donor's and the recipient's blood. Battlefield therapy for shock, burns, and blood loss was revolutionized by the discovery in the 1930s that the plasma portion of blood could be transfused to *anyone* without typing or cross-matching. Plasma is the watery, amber fluid that can be separated by centrifugation from the heavier cellular components (red cells, white cells, and platelets). By 1940 plasma could be prepared in dried form for storage and transport and reconstituted with sterile water for use in field emergencies before moving the patient to a hospital. The U.S. armed services asked the ANRC and the National Research Council in June 1940 to investigate the feasibility of mass plasma production for war purposes and later asked them to furnish a regular blood supply. By 1943 the ANRC had established thirty-five regional and sixty-three mobile donor centers, which collected or distributed 13 million pints for military purposes during the war.[33]

As peace returned, the ANRC looked for new enterprises to sustain its size, idealism, and enthusiasm. Dulles argued that a civilian blood service would be consistent with the Red Cross's tradition of humanitarian and volunteer service without conflicting with government programs. It could also have public relations benefits by "keep[ing] the Red Cross continuously in the minds of those upon whom it depends for support." The project began only after it was approved in principle by the military services, other federal agencies, and various professional health organizations, including the American Medical Association.[34] Apparently the public favored the ANRC's taking on this activity. The Gallup poll in 1947 reported that 73 percent of the persons it sampled favored a national blood program sponsored by the Red Cross and would donate blood to it. It was launched with great enthusiasm in January 1948 but quickly bogged down in some cities, where it encountered strong and unexpected opposition.[35]

Conclusions

Establishing a civilian blood service in 1948 ranks as one of the most important steps in the growth and diversification of the American National Red Cross. At the time the ANRC took on an important function that no other private organization sought except locally and that the U.S. government apparently did not want to perform. Probably few other national organizations then knew more about recruiting blood donors or were better qualified for the task. The venture had public support and was consistent with the ANRC's humanitarian traditions. It was established after an era in which the ANRC had lost ground to rival nonprofit organizations and especially to the federal government. It is not unusual for organizations—either for-profit or nonprofit— to seek growth as a means of achieving greater prestige and improving their prospects for survival. Larger organizations are usually stronger and more difficult for rivals to kill off. Establishing the blood program, therefore, served a variety of Red Cross purposes.

My brief sketch of the ANRC's history to 1950, drawn from Dulles's account, suggests that the move into blood banking was consistent with earlier steps taken by its leaders. Dulles tells the story of a remarkable organization that set consistent goals and knew its self-interests. Its early growth and success were not due simply to its founders' realization that they "bore a great name, [and] had a noble historical background."[36] They were also due to the founders' political skills in obtaining an exclusive franchise and government restraints on the formation of rival organizations authorized to perform similar services—restraints that have long been viewed by economists as important for market control. Later the ANRC diversified in a timely way into new fields where it expected rising demand and relatively little opposition. It pursued diversification even when the new services, such as its ventures into public health and civilian blood supply, were outside the terms of its statutory authority.

Notes

1. American Red Cross, *Annual Report*, 1982, p. 2.
2. "Reagan Notes Red Cross' 100th Anniversary in U.S.," *Los Angeles Times*, February 28, 1981.
3. Foster Rhea Dulles, *The American Red Cross: A History* (New York: Harper and Brothers, 1950), passim.
4. Ibid., p. 340.
5. Ibid., chap. 1; and Martin Gumpert, *Dunant: The Story of the Red Cross* (New York: Oxford University Press, 1938).
6. Gumpert, *Dunant*; and Dulles, *The American Red Cross*, chap. 1.
7. Dulles, *The American Red Cross*, pp. 12.–16.
8. An Act to Incorporate the American National Red Cross, and for other Purposes, U.S. *Statutes at Large*, vol. 31, chap. 784, p. 277 (1900).
9. Dulles, *The American Red Cross*, chap. 4.
10. An Act to Incorporate the American National Red Cross, *Statutes at Large*, vol. 33, pt. 1, chap. 23, p. 599 (1905); and Dulles, *The American Red Cross*, pp. 77–78.
11. To Amend the Act of January 5, 1905, to Incorporate the American National Red Cross, *Statutes at Large*, vol. 61, pt. 1, chap. 50, p. 80 (1947).
12. American Red Cross, *Annual Report, 1983*, p. 33; and interview by telephone with Pat Gilbo, Public Relations Office, American National Red Cross, Washington, D.C., August 1, 1983.
13. *Statutes at Large*, vol. 33, pt. 1, chap. 23, sec. 4, p. 601 (1905).
14. American Red Cross, *Annual Report, 1983*, pp. 21, 25, 30, and annex on Statistical Information.
15. Dulles, *The American Red Cross*, pp. 150, 158.
16. Ibid., pp. 78, 89, 94.
17. Ibid., p. 82.
18. Ibid., pp. 141, 216.
19. Ibid., pp. 307, 366; and interview by telephone with Pat Gilbo, Public Relations Office, American National Red Cross, Washington, D.C., June 1, 1983.
20. Dulles, *The American Red Cross*, p. 18.
21. Ibid., p. 15.
22. Ibid., p. 20.
23. Ibid., p. 21.
24. Ibid., pp. 43, 46–47.
25. Ibid., p. 100.
26. Ibid., pp. 317–18.
27. Ibid., pp. 351–52, 354, 367–68.
28. Ibid., pp. 259, 276–322, 523.
29. Ibid., pp. 356–57, 509.
30. Ibid., p. 99.
31. Ibid., pp. 218–19, 222, 235–38, 251, 253.
32. Ibid., p. 415.
33. Ibid., pp. 413–22.
34. Ibid., pp. 527–29.
35. Ibid., p. 529.
36. Ibid., p. 101.

4
Competition among Blood Collectors

There should be a voluntary, nationwide, nonprofit blood service
with uniform standards of operation—medical, technical, and ad-
ministrative.

BOARD OF GOVERNORS,
American National Red Cross[1]

At a 1975 conference on blood policy at the American Enterprise
Institute, Gordon Tullock suggested that economic self-interest could
explain the efforts of nonprofit blood collectors to discourage for-profit
competitors. He argued that directors of nonprofit organizations, like
their for-profit counterparts, would benefit from greater size, larger
staffs, and the "quiet life" that comes from "acquir[ing] a monopoly."[2]
He also hypothesized that the National Blood Policy's goal of regionalization was a shroud for local cartelization or monopolization.

Tullock's hypotheses are of both academic and policy interest.
Economic analysis appears to explain the interest-group behavior of
both nonprofit and for-profit blood organizations in seeking favorable
regulations or statutes. Economics also helps explain certain deep-
seated rivalries among nonprofit collectors.

The ANRC and the AABB

The U.S. government had asked the American National Red Cross
to undertake its military blood program during World War II and
designated it as the government's blood-collecting agency for both
military and civil defense purposes during the Korean conflict.[3] But
the ANRC shifted to civilian purposes on its own initiative. This led
to jurisdictional disputes with rival blood-banking groups that are
reminiscent of Dulles's account of the problems encountered by the
ANRC when it moved into the public health field in the 1920s.[4]

Until the postwar period, most blood banks were located in hospitals under the influence of staff pathologists. Patients were charged

for blood they did not replace. Almost as soon as the ANRC's plans were announced in 1947, "objections and protests rolled into the American Medical Association headquarters in Chicago from county medical societies which had already set up community banks or were about to do so."[5] They were alarmed by the ANRC's plan to provide zero-priced civilian blood, its leadership by nonphysicians, and its goal of supplying 100 percent of the blood used in the communities it served.

These groups quickly formed the American Association of Blood Banks (AABB). Head-to-head rivalry occurred in some regions, and the ANRC occasionally won because of its zero-priced blood. The American Medical Association tried but failed to mediate jurisdictional boundaries. In 1983 the ANRC had fifty-seven regional blood centers, three-quarters of which were organized by 1954, most by 1962, and the last in 1968. It was strong east of the Mississippi, in Los Angeles, in central California, and in Oregon. By 1971 it collected 47 percent of the country's blood at 1.5 percent of the centers. It took longer than anticipated, however, for the early centers to meet 100 percent of local demand. The AABB preempted the ANRC in the West, the Southwest, and many low-density areas. The AABB also had pockets of strength in Appalachia, in Indianapolis, around New York City, and in Philadelphia. By 1971 32 percent of whole blood was collected by the AABB, 8 percent was drawn at government-owned hospitals, and about 9 percent was bought at commercial centers.[6]

In 1973 the National Blood Policy recognized that neither the ANRC nor the AABB could establish a nationwide system. It proposed to reduce competition between them through regionalization. To implement the policy, the American Blood Commission "acts as a catalyst" to encourage voluntary governance councils called regional associations composed of the "key interest groups"—donors, patients, physicians, hospitals, and blood centers. They "cooperate" by "coordinating" local activities: collecting, processing, and distributing blood and components of the kinds and qualities wanted; managing the regional inventory; disseminating information to the public; and "sharing" donors. The ABC wants especially to cut competition for donors:

> Although it may be appropriate for blood to be collected from donors in more than one blood service unit, the [regional] plan should eliminate conflicting programs for donors by the collecting facilities. Even limited donor recruitment activity by more than one agency acting independently can hamper recruitment efforts for the entire region. . . .
> . . . Conflict between regions will be just as disruptive as

conflict between blood service units within a region.[7]

It is important to include physicians and hospitals as well as organizations that recruit donors in governance councils. Teaching and special-surgery hospitals have a relatively high daily demand for blood and can form rival blood banks if existing collectors serve them poorly. Since the ABC cannot restrict entry, it encourages negotiation, which is often lengthy and acrimonious. As part of its cartelizing efforts, the ABC also attempts to "mediate disputes" over service areas within and between regions. Differential growth rates for populations and hospitals create pressures to change boundaries. Local cartels will be unstable if a region having "excess" donors attracts competition from outside blood banks having "too few."

By 1984 the ABC had approved forty-six regional associations from Maine to Hawaii, accounting for almost half of U.S. blood collections. It expected regional associations to account for 75 percent by 1992. Apparently competition for donors declined where agreements could be reached but continued in other areas, such as Chicago and Washington, D.C.[8]

Monopoly Ambition

In 1960 the ANRC reached a "Statement of Understanding" with the AFL-CIO that recognized their mutual interest in strengthening and expanding the ANRC's nationally coordinated blood program. This agreement also recognized labor's goal of zero-priced blood, a nationwide clearinghouse for donors, and no racial segregation of blood or blood derivatives. After World War II the AFL-CIO operated several blood banks and encouraged its members to donate regularly. In 1971 its executive council called for mandatory labeling of cash blood, prohibition of commercial blood banks, and the development of "a nationally controlled blood program . . . through the American Red Cross, if possible."[9] One year later the ANRC board of governors called for "a voluntary, nationwide, nonprofit blood service with uniform standards of operation—medical, technical, and administrative."[10]

Most organizations, whether for-profit or nonprofit, prefer fewer competitors and, if possible, a monopoly. In this respect the ANRC's position was not unusual. No more than twenty countries delegate full responsibility for whole-blood collection to Red Cross societies, however, and the ANRC's goal was not achieved. Instead of a national blood service it got a National Blood Policy, which was still congenial to its purposes. Cash blood and fees for blood were discouraged. The policy called for collecting data on the plasma markets, which were dominated by for-profit firms. It also expressed doubt about the ap-

42

propriateness in an "all-voluntary system" of the fees to encourage donation that some hospitals and AABB blood banks charged to patients who used more blood than they replaced.[11] The ANRC opposed any rewards to donors as well as disguised blood prices to patients.

The National Blood Policy implicitly sanctioned the agreements that the ANRC made with about 4,000 hospitals in the early 1970s. Under these arrangements the ANRC usually supplied the blood requested (if it was available), and the hospitals received dollar credits for returning out-of-date blood to be salvaged for manufacture. The ANRC charged fees for processing, storage, handling, and transportation, which were passed through to patients along with hospital fees for transfusion services. No fees were to be charged for blood fees did not exceed direct costs. In the 1960s most non-ANRC blood banks and some small hospitals bought some commercial blood because the ANRC had insufficient supplies and rigid rules for ordering blood during off-hours and weekends.[12] The National Blood Policy discouraged such arrangements and probably made these organizations more dependent on the ANRC.

In 1978 the ANRC established an ad hoc committee on blood policy matters to appraise its blood program. After surveying leaders of blood center chapters, the ad hoc group found considerable support for the ANRC's expanding its services and determining an optimal regional service pattern for the country as a whole, even if this could conflict with the activities of the American Blood Commission.[13] By 1979 the ANRC had achieved its goal of providing all the whole blood and components demanded in 75 percent of the regions it served (and in the rest it provided at least 90 percent). It also sought to move into the market for plasma products, which was dominated by commercial fractionators.[14]

The ad hoc committee also thought that the banking of additional tissues would become "an opportunity for future growth." By 1984 the ANRC was attempting to prevent the remuneration of tissue and organ suppliers. About one-sixth of its regional blood centers had begun noncash transplant donation programs. At its 1984 national convention, President Richard F. Schubert announced that the board of governors had approved a plan for the ANRC to increase the supply of tissue and organs: "This is a very natural step for Red Cross to take. Blood is technically a tissue, too. . . . The American Red Cross has the technical, medical and scientific expertise. It has the facilities and the experience necessary for effective donor education and recruitment." The Red Cross's entry into tissue-banking services is consistent with its humanitarian traditions. But it may also be related to the concern that its blood program, in the words of one of its local program directors quoted in an article in the *Wall Street Journal*, "has

43

peaked." In 1984 private and government health insurers paid an estimated $70 million to agencies that found and distributed organs, and they were expected to pay between $200 million and $400 million a year by the end of the decade. Some local, independent transplant and tissue-banking organizations felt threatened by the ANRC's plans, which is reminiscent of the disputes between the ANRC and the AABB after World War II and of the later controversy over cash blood.[15]

Opposing Cash Blood and Tort Liability

In the 1970s the ANRC and the AABB objected to competition between cash blood and noncash blood, although noncash blood might have been expected to do well in such competition where it was in fact of equal or superior quality. Opposition to cash blood remains a unifying force among the ABC and its members. In 1984 the ANRC announced that it still "participates in the national effort to maintain a not-for-profit blood supply that depends on volunteer donors."[16] Undoubtedly some nonprofit blood bankers still believe that cash blood would harm public health. Others may dislike for-profit activity per se. But some may oppose cash blood out of organizational self-interest.

One danger of competition for nonprofit blood bankers is that cash blood would turn out to be of higher quality than they have predicted. I argued in chapter 2 that commercial firms would have incentives to establish brand-name reputations for high-quality blood by using registered and screened suppliers. Demonstrating that cash and noncash blood were at least equally safe would reduce the influence of nonprofit collectors.

A second danger of a dual system is that cash blood would siphon off altruistic donors. Higher prices elicit more production in other areas of economic life and would probably stimulate more nonaltruistic blood suppliers.[17] But higher prices might induce some weakly altruistic donors to cross over to cash buyers.[17] The ANRC is the largest organization specializing in altruistic donors. What would it do if many of those donors responded more to prices than to exhortations for more donations? Competition from for-profit collectors of high-quality cash blood would put the nonprofit organizations in an awkward position owing to their longstanding position in favor of donated blood. How much they would be hurt by for-profit competition is difficult to predict, but surely it is rational for them to worry.

A third danger of competition from cash blood is that it would revive the possibility of assigning tort liability to blood banks for transfusion-associated diseases like hepatitis or AIDS. Kessel's 1974 analysis of the issues and interests still fits:

Eliminating caveat emptor from the blood market would require the current suppliers of blood to adapt to a wholly new set of rules for survival. Whenever liability is placed on the supply side of the medical care market, it is bound to be shifted around so that the supplier of blood will have to effectively guarantee the quality of the product supplied. Hence, standards of supplier responsibility which are characteristic of commercial markets, in particular the drug market, will be imposed upon charitable institutions such as the American Red Cross or hospital blood banks.

Currently the comparative advantage of these organizations in the blood market is solicitation, that is, begging for blood and money. The value of this comparative advantage in a market in which suppliers could not evade product liability would decline sharply; indiscriminate solicitation, because the donor pool is so large, yields too much tainted blood. Hence, imposing strict liability upon these volunteer agencies would be on a par with permitting the practice of nudism only in the polar regions; it is doubtful the cult could survive the rigours of this constraint. Since the supply of blood is the principal product line of the American Red Cross and many other groups, . . . their place in the sun would either be eliminated or sharply reduced. Therefore, it is not difficult to understand why both the hospitals and blood suppliers (and many hospitals are blood suppliers) oppose strict liability.[18]

The ANRC and the AABB declined to endorse a bill introduced in each Congress between 1970 and 1976 by Representative Edward I. Koch (Democrat, New York), to permit taxpayers who donated blood to claim a charitable contribution on their federal income tax returns of $25 per donation to a maximum of $125 per year. The purpose was to reduce shortages and reliance on cash blood by stimulating donations by middle- and upper-income persons.[19] Long ago the Internal Revenue Service ruled that gifts of money or property to charitable organizations are deductible but services (including the time of volunteers) are not. Tax deductions or credits worried the AABB because they "would place a dollar value on blood itself." It wanted to "preserve the principle that the giving of blood is a *service*" [emphasis in original].[20] Making blood a product at law could raise the possibility of creating markets in transplantable organs and tissues. But it could also subject blood banks to strict liability in tort for transfusion-transmitted disease.

The Clearinghouse and the Nonreplacement Fee

Initially the ANRC and the AABB were rivals for blood-banking territories, but by the mid-1970s they were competing mainly for favorable government policies and regulations. The AABB is composed of 2,300 nonprofit hospitals, transfusion centers, and a few large community blood centers. It accredits laboratories, maintains a file on donors of rare blood types, and is the industry's arbiter of technical standards. It also operates the National Clearinghouse to record insurance-like credits that donors can either accumulate against their own future blood use or assign to family and friends in various areas. "The American Association of Blood Banks and its members feel such altruism should be rewarded where possible."[21] "Predeposit credits" against future use cancel nonreplacement fees at hospitals that charge them. This system gives effective price breaks to those who replace blood and help maintain inventories. The AABB also contends that processing fees are lower if blood banks charge for nonreplacement.[22]

The ANRC's philosophy is to make blood available to every patient on the same basis whether or not they have donated to help maintain inventories. It rejects the idea of incentives or rewards of any kind and believes that regular gifts of blood should be everyone's "community responsibility."[23] The ANRC claimed that the National Blood Policy made nonreplacement fees and the AABB's philosophy of "individual responsibility" through blood credits obsolete. Because blood banks no longer had to replace some ANRC blood with allegedly "more expensive" commercial blood, hospitals and blood banks that still used the fee were effectively charging for blood.

Some hospitals charged nonreplacement fees to patients in addition to fees for processing and transfusion whether or not the blood came from banks that charged nonreplacement fees to the hospitals. Most hospitals collected blood only in emergencies, and many got their inventories from the ANRC or other large community blood banks that did not charge for replacement. But most patients put a higher value on blood than these blood banks captured through processing fees. About half the patients without blood insurance paid fees rather than recruit donors. Thus hospitals could increase their incomes by charging nonreplacement fees. This issue eventually split the AABB. Twenty of its largest members opposed the fee, but the AABB's one-bank, one-vote rule meant that it was dominated by hospital banks that wanted the fee. The large banks formed the Council of Community Blood Centers (CCBC) in 1962 and have usually agreed with the ANRC in debates within the ABC.[24]

The ANRC's participation in the AABB's National Clearinghouse initially benefited both organizations. The clearinghouse began in 1953 to keep track of donation credits at blood banks throughout the country, as commercial banks clear checks through the Federal Reserve System. It permitted each AABB member to reward local donors with credits for family or friends who used blood in other communities, including those organized by the ANRC. This gave the decentralized AABB members a broader appeal, such as the ANRC had. ANRC participation increased the number of communities in the clearinghouse network and thus made donation more attractive to ANRC blood centers as well as to AABB members.[25]

In 1972 the ANRC board of governors voted to eliminate all replacement fees and to move toward "community responsibility."[26] In 1976 the ANRC ended its sixteen-year participation in the clearinghouse—a decision probably based partly on ideology. As an ANRC official in Los Angeles County put it, "It is wrong to buy and sell blood like cabbages."[27] But the decision was probably based also on self-interest. The ANRC was usually in deficit to the clearinghouse, a deficit estimated at $300,000 in 1976. The AABB offered to compromise by exchanging only blood instead of cash or credits.[28] But the ANRC refused to have its noncash blood shipped to commercial blood banks occasionally as part of settlement transactions.[29]

Quitting the clearinghouse cost the ANRC good will. Patients hospitalized in communities served by AABB members felt victimized when they were charged replacement fees in spite of having accumulated credits through the ANRC.[30] But its decision also harmed the AABB by making it more difficult for patients in those communities to replace blood if their donors lived in ANRC regions. In 1979 AABB president Byron Myhre told Congress:

> This action was expressly intended to damage a nationwide system for transferral of blood credits and blood itself. Since that time, efforts throughout the country, in State and Federal legislatures and courts, have been initiated to eliminate the credit system of blood banking. These efforts have had an extremely disruptive effect on donor motivation and confidence in our blood banking system.
>
> This matter, which is, frankly, a political problem, deserves further discussion. . . .
>
> The AABB believes that a pluralistic blood supply system is best for a country, such as the United States, which has such diverse characteristics. Although we do not always agree with the Red Cross approach to donor recruitment, we have not attempted to force them to change. We are concerned, however, with efforts directed at our members to usurp self-determinism at the local level and move blood banking toward a single, monolithic system.[31]

The ANRC was perhaps at the peak of its influence when in 1977 the American Blood Commission's board of directors adopted the goal that the U.S. blood supply be "obtained as a community responsibility and without the use of the nonreplacement fee."[32] The AABB was then often isolated in the ABC and opposed a federal charter that could strengthen the organization.[33]

The two rivals also tangled over a Medicare rule that excluded benefits for the first three units of blood used. This rule had been adopted at the AABB's urging to encourage replacement. Some hospitals, however, billed Medicare whether or not blood banks imposed nonreplacement fees. In 1979 Representative Don Edwards (Democrat, California) introduced a bill to end the rule. He predicted this would "encourage hospitals to obtain blood through organizations such as the American Red Cross which do not initially charge blood replacement penalty fees."[34]

In 1979 Senator Richard S. Schweiker (Republican, Pennsylvania) attempted to arbitrate the "civil war in blood" that he blamed for shortages and wasted inventories in some regions.[35] He proposed abolishing the nonreplacement fee and the Medicare exclusion. In place of the clearinghouse he proposed a private national blood exchange that would be open to all collectors but supervised by the U.S. Department of Health and Human Services (HHS). He would have let the AABB give a discount for blood predeposited for the donor's own use of up to 20 percent of the processing fee or the average donor recruitment cost. But Lewellys F. Barker, ANRC blood services vice-president, told Congress:

> We are convinced that the nonreplacement fee will disappear from blood service practice in the United States as more and more blood services turn to the positive motivation of their communities' healthy citizens to be regular blood donors. . . . Americans . . . are ready and willing to donate blood; they need only to be asked and to be given a convenient opportunity to donate.
>
> So the enticement of nonreplacement fee prohibition . . . is not enough to overcome our aversion to the donor discount proposed in the bill. We know from over 40 years' experience with millions of donors that Americans will donate their blood without financial incentive. We believe a financial incentive would cheapen the act of giving one's blood to another who needs it, would tend to place a monetary value on blood and offend countless donors who do not wish or ask to be paid for a gift they are glad to be able to give for those who need blood to regain their health. We know from painful experience with the AABB Clearinghouse that the record-keeping necessary to maintain a national system of donor discounts would be vast and expensive. And if, in the end, all donors became persuaded that they had sufficient credits stored up and no longer needed to donate, the system

would reveal its essential bankruptcy, for there would then be no blood available and all credits would be useless. This is the essence of the fallacy of monetary or paper record incentives to blood donation. They have no meaning without continuing blood donation, which they operate to discourage.[36]

A similar position was taken by HHS. The nonreplacement fee was used in about 33 percent of blood banks in 1979 and had been gradually declining.[37]

Ambition in the Plasma Market

Blood is about one-fourteenth of body weight. It consists of three types of living tissue—red cells to transport oxygen, white cells to fight infections, and platelets to control bleeding—plus plasma. Plasma is the amber, noncellular fluid that constitutes slightly over half of blood volume. It transports cells, hormones, water, and waste products through the circulatory system and contains the proteins that are vital for immune and coagulation processes.

Whole blood is mainly transfused to patients with severe anemias, babies with Rh disease, victims of accident trauma, and surgery patients with huge blood loss. These units probably account for only 20 percent of all donated blood. The rest is used to make packs of red, white, or platelet cells for most surgery and blood therapy and to make products from the plasma.

Demand has increased most for plasma products: clotting-factor concentrates for various blood disorders; serum albumin to expand blood volume for shock and burn victims; gamma globulin to help prevent measles and other infectious diseases; hepatitis B vaccine; and diagnostic materials for medical laboratories.[38] Plasma products do not require blood typing and have longer shelf lives, and some do not transmit hepatitis B. World sales in 1979 exceeded $1 billion and then were growing at 10 to 14 percent per year.[39]

Plasma is obtained by centrifuging whole blood, enabling the lighter plasma to be removed from the heavier, cellular materials. Nonprofit blood collectors obtain plasma as a byproduct of their main activity of providing single-donor units of noncash blood or components for transfusion. Commercial firms collect it by plasmapheresis. After plasma is removed by centrifugation, the cellular materials are returned to the donor by the same intravenous tubing. The whole-blood donor gives up both plasma and cellular materials, which take several weeks to regenerate. But since plasmapheresis takes only plasma, which is regenerated in hours, the process may be repeated three times a week, rather than the maximum five or six times a year

49

for whole-blood donations. Plasmapheresis now requires at least two hours to complete, whereas blood donation takes about thirty minutes. The current annual demand for plasma products—even within the United States—requires much more plasma than noncash donors are willing to provide, given present technologies for plasma collection and processing.

Cash plasmapheresis is not discouraged by the National Blood Policy. In 1981 it was estimated that the average U.S. plasmapheresis supplier gave thirty-five times per year.[40] U.S. firms collect over 60 percent of the world's plasma and manufacture over 70 percent of the world's plasma products. In 1984 plasma was collected at 336 centers in this country, of which 317 were operated by commercial firms paying cash and 19 were operated by nonprofit organizations using noncash donors. In 1981 almost 40 percent of the cash centers were in shopping, residential, or college areas, and 45 percent were in cities of fewer than 500,000 population.[41]

During its 1982–1983 fiscal year, the ANRC collected 6.2 million units of blood, which were used to make 14.3 million transfusible products. Packs of red, white, or platelet cells for transfusion were processed at the laboratories of its regional blood centers. The plasma it collected from whole-blood donations was used to manufacture products that it sold. The ANRC states that revenues from blood services fees may not be used to cross-subsidize its other activities.[42] Apparently higher fees would permit blood services to expand but could lead the United Way to reduce the support it gives for other ANRC programs.[43]

The ANRC's share of the market for plasma products might increase if plasmapheresis appealed to more noncash donors. This would require reducing a two-hour process to perhaps thirty minutes. New plasmapheresis equipment has been developed, but the pumps are not portable, economical, fast enough, or licensed by the Food and Drug Administration. Their effect on the donor's blood cells is unclear, and donors find them less attractive because they require larger needles or two venipunctures.[44] The ANRC's market share might also rise if the manufacturing yield from each batch of plasma could be increased. In 1981 Barker said that if a new method of processing could be found"the American Red Cross and other voluntary blood service organizations could meet all U.S. plasma derivatives needs as part of their comprehensive community blood services."[45]

In the late 1970s the ANRC's plasma products were manufactured under contract by the laboratories of a few state health departments and four commercial fractionators.[46] In 1978 the ANRC announced as a substitute for these transactions joint plans with one of the fractionators to build a $50 million plant with a 1-million-liter annual capacity. Its partner was to have been Baxter-Travenol Laboratories, the principal supplier of plastic blood donation bags and other software used throughout the blood-banking industry. The plant's sole function would have been processing—each partner's collection and marketing functions would have remained separate. Each partner's raw materials were to be processed separately to avoid commingling cash and noncash plasma. The ANRC could have appointed a majority of directors, sold with royalties all technology developed at the plant, and purchased its partner's half interest in the enterprise after ten years.[47] These details of the agreement appear to have been very businesslike.

In 1979 Barker told a U.S. Senate subcommittee, "We hope and trust that there will be a long-range movement toward a voluntary donor base for plasmapheresis."[48] Also in 1979, at a meeting of the American Blood Resources Association (ABRA), Barker was asked: "If the data indicate the incidence of HBsAg is less in commercial center *A* than in Red Cross Center *X*, will the Red Cross use center *A* plasma in its fractionation plant and reject center *X*?" Barker replied: "The answer is NO."[49] In 1980 the ANRC board of governors announced that in addition to its longstanding goal of meeting 100 percent of the needs for whole blood and blood components of the hospitals in each of its regions, it would also meet the region's needs for plasma derivatives to "the fullest extent possible."[50]

The ABRA argued that the proposed joint venture would reduce competition. The ANRC asked the U.S. Department of Justice to review the antitrust implications for the transaction, but the department decided not to challenge it. The plans were canceled in late 1979 owing to unfavorable "current economic conditions."[51] Apparently commercial factors affected plans for the joint venture at each step in the process.

Conclusions

The behavior of each type of blood- or plasma-collecting organization, whether nonprofit or for-profit, appears to have been influenced by its economic self-interest. The ANRC has worked on several fronts, without success, to secure a nationwide monopoly in blood banking with as much governmental support to sanction it as possible. Its attempts to stamp out competition from cash blood have helped to entrench its market position as the dominant organization specializing in the collection of noncash blood. It has opposed using cash blood that was of higher quality than noncash blood. It has supported policies or regulations that favored its operations over nonprofit competitors in a manner reminiscent of its early history. Its withdrawal from the National Clearinghouse weakened the AABB. It considered moving into the direct manufacture of plasma products when demand for them was rising in the late 1970s. It has moved into the noncash supply of tissues and organs and opposed private contracts for them between suppliers and patients.

The ANRC's ideology and economic self-interest fit together well. Many of its actions are consistent with its ideological opposition to buying or charging for whole blood even in subtle ways (although it is not ideologically opposed to selling products it has had manufactured from donated plasma). Many organizations, of course, would like a monopoly, but few for-profit firms attempt to achieve one. Even fewer succeed, owing to costs of excluding rivals without government support. Most blood and plasma collectors have lobbied as interest groups for favorable governmental policies and regulations, and the ANRC has done relatively well in this type of competition.

My description of the Red Cross as coveting plasma markets, selling certain products while giving away services, and organizing its blood services to generate more revenues than costs in 1982–1983 may not fit the picture that some of its donors of blood or other gifts have in mind. To point out that the ANRC engages to some degree in commercial activities is not of itself a criticism. Its plasma activities, for example, may benefit consumers by increasing competition. By the same token, competition from other organizations would benefit patients who receive blood or blood components now provided by the ANRC or AABB nonprofit blood collectors essentially without competition.

Notes

1. American National Red Cross, Board of Governors, "Essential Features of a National Blood Service" (1972).

2. Gordon Tullock, "Commentary," in David B. Johnson, ed., *Blood Policy: Issues and Alternatives* (Washington, D.C.: American Enterprise Institute, 1977), p. 154.

3. Foster Rhea Dulles, *The American Red Cross: A History* (New York: Harper and Brothers, 1950), pp. 413–22. See also statement of Sam T. Gibson, director, ANRC Blood Program, in U.S. Congress, Senate, *Blood Banks and Antitrust Laws, Hearings before the Subcommittee on Antitrust and Monopoly of the Committee on the Judiciary, Pursuant to S. Res. 262 on S. 2560*, 88th Congress, 2d session, August 1964, p. 62; and statement of Frederic S. Laise, ANRC vice-president, in U.S. Congress, Senate, *Proposed Antitrust Exemption for Certain Blood Banks, Hearing before the Subcommittee on Antitrust and Monopoly of the Committee on the Judiciary, Pursuant to S. Res. 26 on S. 1945*, 90th Congress, 1st session, August 1, 1967, pp. 25, 106–7.

4. Dulles, *The American Red Cross*, p. 222.

5. Louanne Kennedy, "Community Blood Banking in the United States from 1937–1975: Organizational Formation, Transformation, and Reform in a Climate of Com-

peting Ideologies" (Ph.D. dissertation, New York University, 1978), p. 95. See also pp. 42, 96–98, chaps. 4–8; Donald E. Brown, "Basic Problem in Blood Banks: Free or Pay," *The Modern Hospital*, May 1955, reprinted in Senate, *Proposed Antitrust Exemption*, pp. 106–14; statement of Frederic S. Laise, ibid., pp. 27, 30; and statement of Sam T. Gibson, director, ANRC Blood Program, in Senate, *Blood Banks and Antitrust Laws*, pp. 66–67.

6. Kennedy, "Community Blood Banking," chap. 3, esp. p. 81.

7. U.S. Department of Health, Education, and Welfare (HEW), Office of the Secretary, "National Blood Policy: Department Responses to Private Sector Implementation Plan," *Federal Register*, vol. 39 (1974), pp. 32702–9; American Blood Commission, *Report of the Task Force on Regional Association of Blood Service Units* (Arlington, Va., 1976), pp. 40–41 and passim; and idem, *American Blood Commission: Program for Regionalization* (Arlington, Va., 1983).

8. Anne R. Lyons, staff associate, American Blood Commission, interviews by telephone, Arlington, Virginia, July 25 and 30, 1984; Emily Friedman, "The Long Road to Regional Blood Programs," *Hospitals*, October 1, 1980, pp. 53–57; S. M. Gaynor and F. Peetoom, "Territorial Issues Addressed through Regionalization," *Transfusion*, vol. 24 (1984), pp. 270–73; and William V. Miller, "Proposed Platform, 1983–84 Officers," Memorandum to American Blood Commission Board of Directors and Members, Arlington, Va., March 11, 1983.

9. "Statement of Understanding between the National Blood Program of the American National Red Cross and the Committee on Community Services of the American Federation of Labor and Congress of Industrial Organizations," October 18, 1960, reprinted in U.S. Public Health Service, National Heart and Lung Institute, National Blood Resource Program, *Supply and Use of the Nation's Blood Resource* (Bethesda, Md.: DHEW Publication no. (NIH) 73-417, 1972), pp. 347–49, exhibit V-9; and AFL-CIO Executive Council, "Statement on Blood Banks," Bal Harbor, Florida, February 16, 1971, reprinted in ibid., exhibit V-10.

10. American National Red Cross, "Essential Features."

11. Alvin W. Drake, Stan N. Finkelstein, and Harvey M. Sapolsky, *The American Blood Supply* (Cambridge, Mass., and London: MIT Press, 1982), p. 121; Piet J. Hagen, *Blood: Gift or Merchandise* (New York: Alan R. Liss, 1982), p. 82; and HEW, Office of the Secretary, "National Blood Policy: Proposed Implementation Plan; Requests for Comments," *Federal Register*, vol. 39 (1974), pp. 9326–30.

12. Kennedy, "Community Blood Banking," p. 115; U.S. Congress, Senate, *Oversight on Implementation of National Blood Policy, 1979, Hearing before the Subcommittee on Health and Scientific Research of the Committee on Labor and Human Resources*, 96th Congress, 1st session, June 7, 1979, pp. 51, 57; Public Health Service, National Blood Resource Program, *Supply and Use of the Nation's Blood Resource*, pp. 113, exhibit IV-3(1), pp. 174–77.

13. American Red Cross, *Report of the Ad Hoc Group on Blood Policy Matters* (Washington, D.C., 1978), pp. 16, 43–44.

14. Senate, *Oversight on National Blood Policy*, pp. 51–53, 57–58; Public Health Service, National Blood Resource Program, *Supply and Use of the Nation's Blood Resource*, pp. 306–7; James Cook, "Blood and Money," *Forbes*, December 11, 1978, p. 37; and Hagen, *Blood*, p. 89.

15. American Red Cross, *Report of the Ad Hoc Group*, p. 33; idem, "News Release: Red Cross against Paid Organ Donors," Washington, D.C., October 28, 1983, pp. 1–2; American Red Cross Blood Services, Los Angeles–Orange Counties Region, *Observer*, June 1, 1984, p. 6; and Michael Waldholz, "Red Cross's Plan to Procure Organs Could Hurt Smaller Organizations," *Wall Street Journal*, August 8, 1984.

16. American Red Cross, "News Release: Statement by Alfred J. Katz, M.D., executive director, American Red Cross Blood Services; for Exclusive Use by *USA Today*," Washington, D.C., National Headquarters, n.d., p. 1.

17. Michael H. Cooper and Anthony J. Culyer, *The Price of Blood*, Hobart Paper 41 (London: Institute of Economic Affairs, 1968), pp. 27–28.

18.   Reuben A. Kessel, "Transfused Blood, Serum Hepatitis, and the Coase Theorem," *Journal of Law and Economics*, vol. 17 (1974), p. 282, copyright 1974, The University of Chicago, and reprinted by permission of the University of Chicago Press; and Richard Landfield, "Some Thoughts about AIDS, Blood Products, and Products Liability Laws," *Plasma Quarterly*, vol. 5 (Fall 1983), pp. 69–70, 88.

19.   U.S. Congress, House, Representative Edward I. Koch speaking for a bill to amend the Internal Revenue Code of 1954 to provide that blood donations be considered charitable contributions deductible from gross income, 91st Congress, 2d session, September 30, 1970, *Congressional Record*, vol. 116, p. 34344; 92d Congress, 1st session, January 21, 1971, *Congressional Record*, vol. 117, pp. 102–3; 92d Congress, 1st session, May 12, 1971, *Congressional Record*, vol. 117, p. 14614; 92d Congress, 1st session, August 5, 1971, *Congressional Record*, vol. 117, pp. 29872–73; 93d Congress, 1st session, September 25, 1973, *Congressional Record*, vol. 119, p. 31398; 93d Congress, 2d session, June 11, 1974, *Congressional Record*, vol. 120, p. 18834; 94th Congress, 2d session, February 9, 1976, *Congressional Record*, vol. 122, pp. 2900–2901; and 94th Congress, 2d session, March 29, 1976, *Congressional Record*, vol. 122, pp. 8472–73. See also U.S. Congress, House, *National Health Insurance Proposals, Hearings before the Committee on Ways and Means*, 92d Congress, 1st session, pt. 12 of 13, November 17 and 18, 1971, pp. 2864–67; and *General Tax Reform, Public Hearings before the Committee on Ways and Means*, 93d Congress, 1st session, pt. 17 of 18, April 16–18, 1973, pp. 6817–21.

20.   American Association of Blood Banks, *AABB Position on Tax Deductions or Credits for Blood Donations* (Arlington, Va., n.d.); and American Blood Commission, "News Release," Arlington, Va., June 7, 1977.

21.   Presumably the AABB meant that altruism should be rewarded in ways other than with cash. American Association of Blood Banks, *Before You Donate, You Should Know . . .* (Arlington, Va., n.d.), p. 2; and Drake et al., *American Blood Supply*, pp. 54–56.

22.   American Association of Blood Banks, *AABB Position on Fees for Blood Transfusion* (Arlington, Va., n.d.).

23.   American Red Cross, *What You Should Know about Giving Blood* (ARC 1786, rev. January 1984), p. 4.

24.   Rachel Westbrook, James Warner Bjorkman, and Jerry Rose, *The Nonreplacement Fee Controversy and National Blood Policy* (Boston: Intercollegiate Case Clearing House, Case No. 9-379-713, 1979), pp. 20–22, 53, 57; and Kennedy, "Community Blood Banking," pp. 110–12, 355, 470–71.

25.   Kennedy, "Community Blood Banking," pp. 106–9, 426; David B. Johnson, "The U.S. Market in Blood," in Armen A. Alchian et al., *The Economics of Charity: Essays on the Comparative Economics and Ethics of Giving and Selling, with Applications to Blood* (London: Institute of Economic Affairs, 1973), pp. 159–60; and Bernice M. Hemphill, "AABB National Clearinghouse Blood Program," *Medical Times*, vol. 98 (August 1970), pp. 101–7, reprinted in House, *National Health Insurance Proposals*, pt. 3 of 13, October and November 1971, pp. 730–36.

26.   American Red Cross, *Who Needs Credit? How Your Blood Service Has Evolved to Serve You and Your Community* (Blood Services, Los Angeles–Orange Counties Region, Form 5334, October 1980), pp. 2–3.

27.   Harry Nelson, "Red Cross Cancels Blood Credits Pact," *Los Angeles Times*, November 5, 1976.

28.   Westbrook et al., *Nonreplacement Fee Controversy*, pp. 46–48; and American Association of Blood Banks, "Red Cross Responds to AABB Blood Cooperative Invitation," *AABB News Briefs*, February 23, 1979.

29.   Statement of Lewellys Barker, ANRC vice-president, in Senate, *Oversight on National Blood Policy*, p. 54.

30.   Nelson, "Red Cross Cancels Blood Credits Pact."

31.   Senate, *Oversight on National Blood Policy*, p. 62.

32. Westbrook et al., *Nonreplacement Fee Controversy*, p. 90; and Drake et al., *American Blood Supply*, pp. 132–33.

33. Kennedy, "Community Blood Banking," pp. 126, 424.

34. American Association of Blood Banks, "Congress Returns: Action on Edwards Bill Due," *Governmental Affairs Newsletter*, September 7, 1979, p. 1; idem, "Subcommittee Rejects Blood Deductible," *AABB News Briefs*, October 1, 1979, p. 4; Westbrook et al., *Nonreplacement Fee Controversy*, pp. 26–27, 30; and U.S. Congress, House, *Amendments to the Medicare Program, Hearings before the Subcommittee on Health of the Committee on Ways and Means*, 96th Congress, 1st session, Serial 96–29, June 18 and 27, 1979, pp. 22–29.

35. Senate, *Oversight on National Blood Policy*, p. 102.

36. U.S. Congress, Senate, *Blood Assurance Act of 1979, Hearing before the Subcommittee on Health and Scientific Research of the Committee on Labor and Human Resources, on S. 1610*, 96th Congress, 2d session, May 1980, p. 45; American Association of Blood Banks, "Senator Schweiker Introduces Bill S-1610," *Governmental Affairs Newsletter*, July 31, 1979; and idem, "AABB Issues Formal Response to Schweiker Legislation," *AABB News Briefs*, September 1, 1979.

37. Testimony of Susanne Stoiber, deputy assistant secretary for health planning and evaluation, U.S. Department of Health and Human Services, in Senate, *Blood Assurance Act*, pp. 10, 88–89; House, *Amendments to the Medicare Program*, p. 431; and Kennedy, "Community Blood Banking," p. 472.

38. Hagen, *Blood*, pp. 13–17.

39. Cook, "Blood and Money," p. 38; and Drake et al., *American Blood Supply*, pp. 71–73.

40. Hagen, *Blood*, p. 189.

41. "Who Collects Plasma?" *Plasma Quarterly*, vol. 6 (Summer 1984), pp. 36–38; "1981 Listing of Source Plasma Licensed Locations," *Plasma Quarterly*, vol. 3 (June 1981), pp. 42–43, 51–60; Vernon Fahle, "The Source Plasma Industry: Statistical Report, 1979," *Plasma Quarterly*, vol. 3 (September 1981), pp. 68–69, 91–94; Robert W. Reilly, "Speak Out! What's Going On in the Plasma Industry?" *Plasma Quarterly*, vol. 3 (June 1981), pp. 36–37, 81–82; and Drake et al., *American Blood Supply*, pp. 122–23.

42. American Red Cross, *Annual Report, 1982*, p. 25.

43. Drake et al., *American Blood Supply*, p. 59.

44. Kenneth Abramowitz, "Economics of Automation: Projected Impact of Automated Plasmapheresis on Plasma Collectors and Fractionators in the 1980's," *Plasma Quarterly*, vol. 1 (June 1979), p. 41; Ronald Williams, "Overview of New Plasmapheresis Automation Technology," *Plasma Quarterly*, vol. 6 (Spring 1984), pp. 20–23; Lynn Hyman, "The Economics of Plasmapheresis by Automation: Revisited," *Plasma Quarterly*, vol. 6 (Spring 1984), pp. 23–24; William Bayer, "Current Experience in an Automated Plasma Collection Program," *Plasma Quarterly*, vol. 6 (Spring 1984), pp. 25–27; and Joseph C. Fratantoni, "Discussion—Perspective of Where Automation Is Going," *Plasma Quarterly*, vol. 6 (Spring 1984), pp. 28–32.

45. "Barker to Symposium: Voluntary Donor-Based AHF Supply within Reach," *American Red Cross Blood Services Bulletin*, June 8, 1981, p. 1.

46. Cook, "Blood and Money," p. 38; Thomas C. Drees, "Worldwide Plasma Supply and Demand," in Robert L. Crouch, ed., *Plasma Forum: A Public Exchange of Views Regarding Plasmapheresis Sponsored by the American Blood Resources Association* (McNally and Loftin, West, 1979), p. 6; and "The Red Cross: Drawing Blood from Its Rivals," *Business Week*, September 11, 1978, p. 113.

47. Cook, "Blood and Money," p. 38; Richard Landfield, "A Quick Look at the Joint Venture," *Plasma Quarterly*, vol. 1 (February 1979), pp. 11, 28–29; and "Red Cross Plasma Business and Federal Taxes," *Plasma Quarterly*, vol. 1 (December 1979), pp. 100–101.

48. Senate, *Oversight on National Blood Policy,* p. 58.

49. W. L. Warner, ed., *Plasma Forum: February 26–27, 1979; A Public Exchange of Views Regarding Plasmapheresis* (American Blood Resources Association, n.d.), p. 214.

50. Hagen, *Blood,* pp. 89–91.

51. "The Red Cross: Drawing Blood from Its Rivals," p. 113; Robert W. Reilly, executive director, American Blood Resources Association, letter to Charles V. Reilly, U.S. Department of Justice, Antitrust Division, New York Regional Office, "Comments on Proposed Joint Venture between American National Red Cross and Baxter-Travenol Laboratories, Inc.," June 20, 1978, p. 18, n. 14; U.S. Department of Justice, "News Release," October 27, 1978; John H. Shenefield, assistant attorney general, Antitrust Division, letter to George Elsey, president, American National Red Cross, Washington, D.C., October 27, 1978; and Elsey, telex to field office managers, division managers, and regional directors, American Red Cross Blood Services, November 29, 1979.

5
The AIDS Crisis

The voluntary blood supply in the United States is safer than ever before.

WILLIAM V. MILLER, President,
American Blood Commission[1]

Red Cross and others who collect blood are committed to maintaining the safest blood supply possible. We will help advance medical knowledge and will respond to new information as it becomes available.

ALFRED J. KATZ, Executive Director,
American Red Cross Blood Services[2]

The acquired immune deficiency syndrome (AIDS) is a lethal new disease that is transmitted by blood transfusion among other ways. It quickly became what is probably the most controversial public health problem in our nation's history.

AIDS was spread by blood transfusion more widely and quickly than was necessary owing to the failure of blood and plasma collectors to adopt registries over a decade ago, when hepatitis was the worst transfusion-transmitted disease. As AIDS spread, both groups again failed to establish registries. The rules established by nonprofit blood collectors for screening noncash blood donors differed, however, from those established by for-profit manufacturers of plasma products for screening cash plasma suppliers. This difference provided a natural test case for my thesis that more competition in blood banking would improve the blood collected to the quality that consumers have indicated they prefer.

Another Viral Connection

AIDS was first observed in Haiti in 1978 and in New York City in 1979 and was reported by the U.S. Centers for Disease Control (CDC) in spring 1981. In June 1983 Margaret Heckler, secretary of health and human services, declared it the government's "number one health priority."[3]

AIDS occurs when a certain group of white blood cells is no longer effective in protecting the body from invading pathogens. Victims succumb to a series of severe pneumonias or other bacterial, viral, fungal, or protozoal infections caused by germs that are ordinarily harmless to healthy people, as well as to a rare type of cancer. These "marker" diseases along with characteristic white-cell abnormalities are used to define AIDS pending the discovery of its agent. By June 18, 1984, 4,918 cases and 2,221 deaths of adults, adolescents or children in forty-five states, the District of Columbia, and Puerto Rico had been reported to CDC. By early 1984 over 76 percent of those diagnosed before July 1982 and almost 90 percent of those diagnosed in 1980 had died. New cases were reported at the rate of about ten per day. The onset of symptoms of AIDS is often very gradual, and its insidious and variable incubation period makes its future scope uncertain. The average patient requires two to three months of hospitalization. Another 2,000 cases could cost $100 million.

CDC statistics include only full-blown AIDS cases. They exclude borderline cases and persons with immune-system suppression who have not developed one of the marker diseases. Persons with "pre-AIDS" white-cell abnormalities are believed to outnumber the confirmed AIDS cases by a factor of ten. Similar abnormalities can be caused, however, by transient viral infections of several kinds. Until the AIDS agent is identified, there is no way to tell which pre-AIDS persons will develop the full syndrome.

AIDS was first thought to be a venereal condition among highly promiscuous male homosexuals and bisexuals, but it was later found in other groups. By June 1984 homosexual and bisexual males constituted about 72 percent of adult cases, intravenous drug abusers over 17 percent, persons from Haiti now living in the United States 4 percent, persons with hemophilia almost 1 percent, heterosexual contacts of persons at increased risk for AIDS about 1 percent, and recipients of blood transfusions about 1 percent. These percentages have remained relatively constant as reported cases have increased. Unusual cases of immune disease in Europe and equatorial Africa before 1981 are now believed to have been AIDS.[4] AIDS has also developed in wives of persons in high-risk groups, female prostitutes, newborn children of parents with AIDS, children living in households of persons with AIDS, and a few hospital workers.[5]

The first transfusion-associated case occurred in December 1982. A San Francisco infant who was not in any other high-risk group was transfused for Rh incompatibility at two weeks of age and died of AIDS at twenty months. One of the child's noncash donors to a nonprofit blood bank who belonged to a high-risk group was well at the time of donation but died eighteen months later of full-blown AIDS.[6] Of fifty-seven pediatric cases of AIDS reported through June 18, 1984, twelve had transfusions with blood or blood components before their onsets of illness. Premature infants, perhaps because of partially developed immune systems, seem particularly vulnerable. For this reason CDC statistics initially excluded pediatric cases under five years of age; now pediatric cases are reported separately from adults.[7] A conclusive adult case was that of a thirty-eight-year-old Los Angeles woman who in December 1983 received two units of blood from two donors. Two months later one of her donors was identified as a high-risk person who had been hospitalized with AIDS. The woman was hospitalized with AIDS thirteen months after the transfusion. Another woman transfused with the same donor's blood was asymptomatic in early 1984 but had abnormal white cells.[8]

A study published in the *New England Journal of Medicine* in January 1984 found that almost 1 percent of 2,157 patients with AIDS had no recognized risk factors other than transfusion. These eighteen patients received blood from two to forty-eight donors (median, fourteen), 10 to 43 months (median, 24.5) before the onset of AIDS. None of the donors had developed AIDS by the time the study was published. But six of seven AIDS patients in the group who were studied in detail had been exposed to at least one donor from a high-risk group, and all seven were exposed to donors with pre-AIDS blood abnormalities. The article concluded that "these findings strengthen the evidence that AIDS may be transmitted in blood."[9] By June 18, 1984, AIDS had been found in sixty-four transfusion recipients, in addition to thirty-eight hemophiliacs (for whom AIDS was the second leading cause of death in 1982).[10]

It was suspected from the outset that AIDS was viral because its epidemiology was similar to that of hepatitis B. AIDS also appeared to have an incubation period or carrier state in which persons with infectious disease were well enough to donate blood. In May 1984, three years after the first AIDS case was reported, Robert C. Gallo and his associates of the National Cancer Institute of the U.S. National Institutes of Health claimed to have isolated its agent. They found antibodies to a rare virus in forty-three of forty-nine AIDS victims and eleven of fourteen persons with pre-AIDS abnormalities. French scientists earlier claimed to have isolated a rare virus from AIDS victims, which may prove to be the same virus the Gallo group found in spite of its different name. The techniques employed by the French scientists were used to isolate a virus from the blood of the Los Angeles woman and her donor mentioned earlier, both of whom had AIDS— strong evidence that AIDS was transmitted by transfusion. It was hoped that a screening test based on the Gallo group's techniques would be ready by early 1985. But even if the virus they found is in fact the AIDS agent, a vaccine is still several years away, owing to the difficulty of working with and testing materials capable of causing cancer.[11]

Screening Some Dangerous Donors

AIDS has been called the greatest epidemic since poliomyelitis. As with most communicable diseases, a partial but immediate counter-measure is to narrow the range of contact among high-risk persons and between high-risk groups and the general population. During epidemics of polio, for example, public health authorities closed schools and discouraged large gatherings at theaters and public swimming pools. Persons vulnerable to nontransfusion AIDS can adjust their behavior to reduce risks, but persons at transfusion risk for AIDS have fewer choices. Because local blood banks are usually noncom-petitive, it is difficult for patients to shop for better blood as they do for physicians and most consumer goods. Some persons facing elec-tive surgery can deposit their own blood in advance for what is called an autologous transfusion. But patients in emergencies and those needing many units must rely on blood collectors to screen donors carefully.

New screening procedures were developed in late 1982 and early 1983, shortly after the San Francisco infant's death was publicized. The U.S. Public Health Service defined high-risk blood donors as persons with symptoms suggestive of AIDS, sexually active homo-sexual or bisexual men, Haitian entrants to the United States and persons who had recently visited Haiti, patients with hemophilia, present or past abusers of intravenous drugs, and sexual partners of either AIDS patients or persons at greater risk for AIDS.[12] On January 14, 1983, the National Hemophilia Foundation asked manufacturers of clotting-factor concentrates for hemophilia patients to (1) exclude all high-risk suppliers by direct questioning, (2) close collection cen-ters in areas populated by high-risk persons, (3) cease buying plasma from any collector that did not exclude high-risk suppliers, and (4) make more products from the plasma of one person rather than from pools of perhaps thousands of persons.[13]

The commercial manufacturers of these products had already begun to purchase plasma from lower-risk suppliers. Alpha Thera-peutic Corporation stopped purchasing plasma in Los Angeles, New York, and San Francisco on December 10, 1982, and other firms soon followed suit in these cities and Miami in cooperation with the Food and Drug Administration. On December 21, 1982, Alpha began to interrogate each potential plasma supplier on each visit about whether he or she was in a high-risk group or was in contact with persons in such groups. On January 1, 1983, Alpha stopped purchasing plasma from any blood bank that screened less rigorously than Alpha did at its own plasma-collection centers.[14]

On January 28, 1983, the American Blood Resources Association recommended that commercial fractionators "discourage high risk individuals from [supplying] . . . plasma." Suppliers should be questioned about symptoms and possible contacts with persons having AIDS, required to acknowledge in writing that they were not members of high-risk groups, and given physical examinations for AIDS signs at the first visit and regularly thereafter.[15] This policy was approved by the FDA.[16] Fractionators recalled products found to contain plasma from persons who later developed AIDS, as did the American National Red Cross (ANRC).[17]

Disagreements between the for-profit and nonprofit collectors over standards for screening donors emerged in the commentary at an ad hoc meeting for worried groups that the Centers for Disease Control held in Atlanta on January 4, 1983. Clyde McAuley of Alpha Therapeutic Corporation said they would exclude plasma from all high-risk groups "because frankly we don't have anything else to offer at this time." Michael Rodell of the Pharmaceutical Manufacturers Association said, "The rest of the plasmapheresis industry is in various stages of instituting a program like Alpha's."

Representatives of some nonprofit blood banks disagreed. Aaron Kellner of the New York Blood Center said: "Don't overstate the facts. There are, at most, three cases of AIDS from blood donations, and the evidence in two of these cases is very soft. And there are only a handful of cases among hemophiliacs." Joseph Bove, director of the Yale–New Haven Blood Bank and chairman of the Committee on Transfusion-Transmitted Disease of the American Association of Blood Banks (AABB), said: "We are contemplating all these wide-ranging measures because one baby got AIDS after transfusion from a person who later came down with AIDS and there may be a few other cases." Jeffrey Koplan, CDC assistant director, told Bove: "To bury our heads in the sand and say 'Let's wait for more cases' is not an adequate public health measure." Donald Armstrong of Memorial Sloan-Kettering Cancer Center in New York, who has treated many AIDS victims, said: "I have absolutely no doubt that AIDS is transmitted by sex and blood products." David Sencer of the New York City Health Department agreed: "Does anyone doubt that we are dealing with an infectious agent that is transmitted by blood and sexual contacts?"[18]

61

On January 13, 1983, about a week after the ad hoc meeting, the ANRC, the AABB, and the Council of Community Blood Centers (CCBC) adopted a joint statement on high-risk donors. It said that evidence for transfusion-transmitted AIDS was "inconclusive" and "incomplete"[19] (Gallo's work was published eighteen months later) and reflected the caution expressed by Kellner and Bove. The three organizations adopted weaker screening standards for high-risk donors than the commercial fractionators. The FDA approved their joint policy, which remained in force in April 1984.

ANRC blood centers and AABB member blood banks have routinely given prospective donors a "miniphysical" examination consisting of a short medical history, weight, temperature, pulse, blood pressure, and hemoglobin level from a droplet of blood taken from the finger tip or ear lobe. It was also standard practice to check donors' arms for evidence of needle sticks and to test each unit of blood for syphilis and HBsAg. Apparently these procedures were not changed in the wake of AIDS. Prospective donors were not examined for swollen lymph nodes or other signs of AIDS as ABRA recommended and the FDA approved for collectors of cash plasma.[20]

Beginning early in 1983 prospective Red Cross donors were handed brochures describing AIDS symptoms and signs, how it is spread, persons at risk, and warning of the dangers of donating blood if they had this condition or had contact with persons who had it. Before donating they were asked to sign a statement indicating that they understood what they had read. Persons who believed that they were at risk of AIDS were asked to refrain from donating or, if they wanted more information, to ask questions of a Red Cross nurse or physician during the health history interview.[21] Beginning in April 1983 the AABB recommended that its members distribute similar literature and asked their donors to acknowledge in writing that they had read it and understood that members of high-risk groups had been asked not to donate.[22]

ANRC blood centers were required by national headquarters to expand the health history interview beyond routine questions about hepatitis, malaria, and self-injected drugs to include questions designed to detect persons who had symptoms of AIDS or had been exposed to persons who might have AIDS. They were told, however, that "at this time, there should be no direct questions concerning a donor's sexual preference; nor should a donor be asked to self-exclude on this basis." These health history questions would screen persons who had been to Haiti, had been hospitalized recently, or were obviously ill. Moreover, donor recruiters were told that they "should not target recruitment efforts toward groups that may have a high incidence of AIDS."[23] Staff nurses in the ANRC Los Angeles–Orange counties region were told that prospective donors who did not exclude themselves after reading the information brochure but requested a nurse's advice after volunteering that they belonged to a high-risk group could be advised not to donate blood until a definitive screening test for AIDS is devised. The blood of such persons who insisted on donating was to be used "for research."[24]

These screening procedures were probably of some benefit; how much will not be known for some time. But they did not discourage high-risk donors or attempt to exclude them categorically. In many cases the decision whether to donate was left up to the judgment, sophistication, and good will of the donor alone, although staff nurses could unofficially defer more donors than usual for such minor complaints as tiredness or a poor night's sleep. Ending outright solicitation of high-risk AIDS groups was most welcome. But officials of the ANRC and all other collectors of blood or plasma (cash or noncash) should also have screened out hospital workers and other high-risk groups for non-A, non-B hepatitis, which cannot be detected by specific blood tests.

What should have been obvious was that these procedures would not prevent some contaminated blood from slipping through. Before being diagnosed as having AIDS, a person in Sacramento donated blood eleven times between 1979 and February 1983, and a person in the San Francisco Bay area donated thirteen times between January 1980 and July 1983. The first person donated once after the new screening procedures were implemented, and the second person donated twice. Five of the second person's donations to the Peninsula Blood Bank were used for direct transfusion. Seven donations to the Red Cross in San Jose were either used for direct transfusion or sent to Baxter-Travenol Laboratories (the firm with which the ANRC considered a joint venture) for manufacture into plasma products, which were eventually sold to patients. Nine of the twelve patients directly transfused with this person's blood died of the primary diseases for which they were originally diagnosed. Of the three living in April 1984, one was a kidney patient, one had pre-AIDS white-cell abnormalities, and one had not been tested.

The single unit donated by the second person to the Stanford University Medical Center was destroyed before it could be used for any purpose because it had T-cell abnormalities. The T-cell test indicates reduced natural immunity, which is common in persons with AIDS or pre-AIDS (but also in some healthy persons). In 1984 few blood banks other than Stanford's used the T-cell test as a standard operating procedure.[25]

Potentially tragic errors like those in northern California were acknowledged in March 1984 by Bove: "There have been some slip-ups in the screening program; that's going to happen in any such situation."[26] Perhaps it was realized at the outset that the new screening procedures erred on the side of risk. John C. Petricciani, director of the FDA Office of Biologics, which approved them, said: "It's not going to be 100 percent effective; everyone knows that. . . . At the same time, we're hopeful it will have an impact."[27]

Others recommended tighter screening. Richard Digioia, chairman of the District of Columbia Medical Society Committee on Blood and Infectious Diseases, suggested in February 1984 that persons who had received blood before the new screening procedures were instituted and any homosexual or bisexual male who had not been monogamous or celibate for at least four years should not be permitted to donate.[28] It would not have been sensible to exclude female homosexuals, because their blood is believed to be safe. Members of one organization of female homosexuals increased their donations, and others should be encouraged to do so and congratulated when they do.[29] Some commercial firms now make certain products from the plasma of women only.

The practical problem was whether to attempt to exclude all male homosexuals. Gay organizations said that such a policy would be defamatory and might have viewed it as a civil rights issue. The U.S. Department of Health and Human Services opposed it. One of its officials argued that exclusion might alienate some persons to the point of donating out of spite regardless of their health.[30] The joint statement on high-risk donors issued by the ANRC, the AABB, and the CCBC acknowledged that they were under pressure to prevent gay males from donating blood. But they were concerned about violating the privacy of prospective donors for what they believed to be a dubious benefit in reducing the spread of AIDS, which by January 1983, they believed, had not been conclusively linked to transfusion. They preferred to work with leaders of organizations with members in high-risk groups to inform them of the dangers to patients if such members donated and to hold off more stringent measures until they were warranted by new medical or scientific findings.[31]

In the 1970s blood collectors excluded certain groups whom they believed or knew to be high-risk carriers of hepatitis B. Cash blood was denigrated even when it was of higher quality than noncash blood. It was reported in 1977 that the Greater New York Blood Program found that certain minority groups had higher than average rates of HBsAg, and the British National Transfusion Service did not solicit donations from immigrants from Africa, Asia, and the Caribbean.[32] About 10 percent of prospective donors to the ANRC blood services in Los Angeles and Orange counties in early 1984 were disqualified because of their health history. About 3 to 5 percent of all ANRC blood was rejected because of HBsAg in 1983.[33] Neither the for-profit nor the nonprofit collectors, however, have attempted to exclude hospital workers, and it was only after AIDS developed that the for-profit collectors began to exclude male homosexuals (who are also at high risk for hepatitis).

A staff writer for the *Los Angeles Times* inferred in March 1983 that the ANRC adopted a weaker screening policy because "the evidence of transmission of . . . [AIDS] through donated blood was scanty and that the effect on voluntary blood donation might be enormous."[34] A reduction in the amount of whole blood collected would reduce both the ANRC's supply of packed cells for direct transfusion and its supply of plasma for manufacture into various products. The ANRC also realized the possible market implications of transfusion-associated AIDS. Hemophiliacs might increase their demand for single-donor plasma products supplied by the Red Cross over multiple-donor products made by for-profit fractionators. The ANRC expected that "this in turn could lead [for-profit] plasmapheresis establishments to seek amended licenses to permit the production of single donor . . . [products]. Regions should be especially cognizant of the potential for competition for single donor product distribution from this source."[35]

Some blood bankers appeared content with the new screening standards. In early 1984 Alfred J. Katz, executive director of ANRC blood services, said that "we have a very safe and effective blood supply."[36] Assistant director Roger Dodd argued that "the evidence suggests that current screening is as satisfactory as any alternative mechanisms that have been proposed."[37] Bove said in the *New England Journal of Medicine* that "physicians can and should reassure patients that appropriate steps have been taken to prevent members of high-risk groups from being blood donors, with the expectation that eventually this approach will reduce the number of cases."[38] Later Bove claimed that "more people die of bee stings than of transfusion-transmitted AIDS," although the relation between the two types of illness is nil.[39]

Katz also stated that "blood is a medicine and, like any medicine, it has risks as well as benefits."[40] This statement is misleading. The risks of blood incompatibility and human error have surely been minimized by refining techniques and procedures in millions of transfusions. But the risk due to blood bankers' judgments of which donors to reject have deliberately not been minimized. Apparently Katz was referring to the known side effects of certain medicines for some people. But these are not analogous to the risk of transmitting AIDS by failing to screen high-risk donors. The correct analogy between the blood-screening risk and medicines would be to make medicines from raw materials that were likely to convey serious disease when safer substitutes were available. Viewed in this light, commercial firms adopted screening procedures to provide safer raw materials for their patients than the nonprofit blood collectors adopted for the general public.

Opposing Directed Donations

Some patients wanted to circumvent the "potluck" pool of noncash donors in spite of the new screening procedures by asking family and friends to direct donations for their use. A few communities formed "blood clubs" for this purpose.[41] Directed donations were more difficult than they appeared. All units had to be the correct type and had to be obtained before hospitalization. Extra units had to be available to allow for surgical complications or blood incompatibility.[42] These restrictions made directed donation impractical for emergencies, some open-heart procedures, and most transplant surgeries, where many units were needed at once. But with planning it could work for those needing a few units and for some patients who knew that they required transfusion regularly.

A Florida case received national attention in August 1983. A father wanted to donate blood for his son, who was seriously ill with a virus that prevented digestion. The father feared that the child had little remaining natural immunity, and their physician believed that a directed donation was "legitimate and reasonable." But the Central Florida Blood Bank had an "unwritten policy" against it. Representative E. G. (Bud) Shuster (Republican, Pennsylvania) introduced a bill in the Ninety-third Congress to permit it when recommended by a physician. He let the matter drop after the bill was opposed by the three nonprofit blood-collecting organizations.[43]

The AABB, the ANRC, and the CCBC issued a joint statement explaining their opposition. First, they argued:

> The concept that family members, friends, coworkers, church members or other selected groups are sure to provide safer blood is unrealistic. These same individuals are and have been the nation's volunteer blood donors who have, in the past, given freely for all patients rather than for a particular individual. There is no reason to think that segregating these individuals into selected donor panels will provide safety over and above the level provided by current arrangements.[44]

Indeed, no body of evidence showed that friends or family were superior to the 1983 noncash donor pool, but that they were was a reasonable expectation. Patients anticipating transfusion probably read newspaper articles about blood collectors refusing to discourage donors and instances where persons eventually diagnosed as having AIDS had donated in spite of the new screening procedures. A patient in this position naturally would want to err on the side of too much safety rather than too much risk. Patients who selected donors who did not work in hospitals or dental offices would, perhaps without realizing it, also put themselves at lower risk for posttransfusion hepatitis. Patients could choose among physicians, hospitals, and some medicines, so why not among blood donors?

Second, the blood collectors argued that patients might not realize that some of the donors they selected were also in high-risk groups. This could "create intense pressures on . . . [donors to] be untruthful about their ability to meet donor requirements." The same problem would arise, however, for donors solicited by blood collectors through exhortations, blood drives, and peer pressures at workplaces. In early 1984 several blood banks, including an ANRC chapter, established twenty-four-hour telephone lines so that donors in high-risk groups who later regretted having donated could confidentially ask for their blood to be destroyed.[45] These telephone lines could have been used to cancel directed donations just as easily.

Third, directed donations were expected to raise blood-banking costs and to increase the "chance of human error resulting from [a] greater level of special handling by blood collecting and transfusing staffs."[46] Directed donations had to be typed and cross-matched just as others did, but extra transportation and handling might be required to get them to the correct hospitals. What could be the harm in blood banks' providing this service if patients and hospitals were willing to pay for it?

Fourth, blood collectors argued that directed donation "risks the creation of a system which could discriminate against the poor and the elderly."[47] Wealthier patients will not necessarily have more family and friends willing to donate, although younger people may. Moreover, directed donations will probably produce "extra" blood available for anyone's use. Some donations will not match the patient's blood, and some patients will not need all the blood collected for them. (The patient is not likely to want to keep unused blood, and few donors are likely to want it back.)

A few large university-affiliated hospitals with their own blood banks permitted directed donations in 1983. The results at one in Philadelphia were published in the *New England Journal of Medicine.*

The concerns of whole-blood collectors about higher costs and too few donations were the opposite of what happened.

All designated donors are screened in the same manner as random donors. In addition, if the donor's blood is not compatible with the intended recipient's or not used by the intended recipient, it is released for use by another patient. To date 42 patients have participated, with a total of 142 donations. Eighty of the latter were returned to the general blood inventory and transfused to other patients. . . . These 142 donations represent 426 blood products generated within our hospital rather than procured from outside sources. A cost analysis of whole-blood donation documented that at current activity levels, whole blood can be drawn and processed into packed red cells, fresh-frozen plasma, and platelets at a savings of $29.17, as compared with the cost of procuring the same components from an outside source. Thus, this program has resulted in savings to the institution of $4,142 in four months. The annual figure is $12,426—a substantial reduction in operating expenditures.[48]

The authors made no claim about the safety of directed donations.

The three organizations also had "a real concern that donors may refrain from routine blood donations while awaiting requests to provide directed donations and, thereby, could disrupt the blood supply to the point that routine and even some emergency needs for transfusions may go unmet."[49] A New York blood banker said, "If people set up private pools, . . . we'd see little pockets of donors, and eventually the blood banks would be destroyed."[50] Edward O. Carr, president of the AABB and executive director of the Central Florida Blood Bank, said, "Although individual requests to give blood specifically . . . may seem justified on their individual merits, we are compelled to look to the greater good to be served by insuring that a safe supply of voluntarily donated blood is available for all who need it."[51]

A decline in donations and a rise in competitive suppliers offering safer products with more economical collection procedures were the whole-blood collectors' most central and rational fear. I showed in chapter 2 that registries in the 1970s could yield better blood than random collections, and I showed in chapter 4 that blood collectors were concerned about competition. Directed donations amounted to a miniregistry—a noncash "market" to raise the likelihood of getting high-quality blood. Because they were transactions between friends and family who cared about one another rather than transactions between strangers, the incentives for honesty and caution went up rather than down. Transactions between strangers are common throughout our economy, of course. But buyers are usually protected by dealing with competitive sellers, many of whom offer either implied or express warranties for the quality of what they sell, and by knowing that sellers hope to get their custom on future occasions. In the case of whole blood, patients were usually dealing on a one-time basis with noncompetitive collectors that enjoyed legislative exemptions from strict liability in tort. Patients had a natural fear that they were being handed a "product" that was not as safe as it would have been if collectors had had different incentives.

The American Blood Commission also feared the "risk of entrepreneurs, 'blood businesses,' arising to provide a service to patients willing to receive blood from qualified donors and willing to pay a premium for it because they are unable to secure sufficient volunteer blood donors for their blood needs."[52] This statement was probably wrong in suggesting that directed donations would end altruistic donations. But altruistic donations might decline, and marked declines could force blood collectors either to cut back their staffs or to improve the quality of their services so that patients got blood that was just as good as they could get by finding their own donors. The statement was probably accurate in predicting that the market would begin to provide unconventional blood-banking services. Commercial firms in Houston in early 1984 were planning to freeze and store blood for a fee and deliver it anywhere for use by the owner or whoever was designated.[53] Whether there would be sufficient demand for such a firm to start up and survive depends on whether noncompetitive blood collectors eventually offer the type and quality of services that most consumers want.

In June 1984 a major AABB blood bank, Irwin Memorial in San Francisco, began a directed donation program "as a response to public pressure" in a city where many AIDS cases have been found.[54] The procedures required a series of consents not only by the patient and the donor but by the patient's physician and the transfusion service of the hospital where the transfusion would take place. The procedures also required that each donor make two visits to the downtown blood bank—once for prescreening (when a $15 fee must be paid) and again for the donation—rather than just the one visit required of routine donors. (Designated donors were asked to make another donation to the general inventory within one year.) Irwin's requirements were relatively bureaucratic and inconvenient for donors, however, so some patients might not try to comply.

Conclusions

Commercial fractionators attempted to maintain the safety and attractiveness of their products as the AIDS crisis unfolded by purchasing plasma from lower-risk suppliers even if it cost more. They were concerned about the safety of their customers and knew that customers would value the extra protection. Each firm's improvement in product safety would also have to be matched by its competitors. Otherwise the demand for their products would decline as patients consumed less or shifted to single-donor materials produced by the Red Cross and other blood banks.

The nonprofit whole-blood collectors were also concerned about blood quality and the health of patients. But they tried to protect the general public with standards for screening donors that were weaker than those used by for-profit firms. To some degree these standards were influenced by pressure-group politics and fears of losing too many donors. Embarrassing blood shortages might have created pressures for competitive sources of supply.

Whether the whole-blood collectors met their own performance standards as characterized by the quotations at the beginning of this chapter is difficult to say. Their screening standards improved but were not as strong as they could have been or as strong as those the commercial sector adopted. Both groups failed to protect patients to the maximum extent with registries. It was also rare for blood collectors in either group to test blood routinely for T-cell abnormalities or for the hepatitis core antibody. Neither test reveals AIDS specifically, and each is in only its first generation of accuracy. But each would remove some doubtful donors from the pool, especially if used in conjunction with registries. Moreover, the blood of AIDS patients often shows the hepatitis core antibody; so this test is likely to help remove some filth of each kind from the blood supply.

Whether the general public has been well protected from transfusion-transmitted AIDS will still be relevant if a foolproof test for the AIDS agent or agents is developed soon and even if AIDS is eradicated. The variety of planetary life is colossal, and viruses mutate naturally, as the AIDS virus may have done. Something like AIDS could occur every generation or so and be spread quickly by blood transfusion before tests or vaccines are devised. Prevention of such illnesses requires registries.

Notes

1. William V. Miller, *A Message to American Blood Commission Members about AIDS and Transfusion* (Arlington, Va.: American Blood Commission, 1983).

2. Alfred J. Katz, "Blood's Value Far Exceeds Risks," *USA Today*, March 23, 1984.

3. "Heckler Tells Mayors of AIDS Battle Plan," *Los Angeles Times*, June 15, 1983; U.S. Congress, House, *The Federal Response to AIDS, Twenty-ninth Report by the Committee on Government Operations, Together with Dissenting and Additional Views*, H. Rept. 98-582, 98th Congress, 1st session, November 30, 1983, pp. 3–4.

4. As this was written in June 1984, information on AIDS cases and research was still moving rapidly. From a large literature, see American Red Cross, Los Angeles–Orange Counties Regional Blood Services, *Observer*, June 1, 1984, p. 2; "Battling a Deadly New Epidemic," *Time*, March 28, 1983, pp. 53–55; James W. Curran, "AIDS—Two Years Later," *New England Journal of Medicine*, vol. 309 (1983), p. 609; Harry Nelson, "Doctors Face Ethical Dilemma on AIDS Virus Tests," *Los Angeles Times*, June 29, 1984; U.S. Congress, Congressional Research Service, *AIDS: Acquired Immune Deficiency Syndrome* (Washington, D.C.: Library of Congress, Issue Brief No. IB83162, by Judith A. Johnson, rev. March 27, 1984); and U.S. Public Health Service, Centers for Disease Control, "Update: Acquired Immunodeficiency Syndrome (AIDS)—United States," *Morbidity and Mortality Weekly Report*, vol. 33 (1984), pp. 337–39.

5. Anthony S. Fauci, "The Acquired Immune Deficiency Syndrome: The Ever-Broadening Clinical Spectrum," *Journal of the American Medical Association*, vol. 249 (1983), pp. 2375–76; Carol Harris et al., "Immunodeficiency in Female Sexual Partners of Men with the Acquired Immunodeficiency Syndrome," *New England Journal of Medicine*, vol. 308 (1983), pp. 1181–84; and "New Theories about AIDS," *Newsweek*, January 30, 1984, p. 50.

6. U.S. Public Health Service, Centers for Disease Control, "Possible Transfusion-Associated Acquired Immune Deficiency Syndrome (AIDS)—California," *Morbidity and Mortality Weekly Report*, vol. 31 (1982), pp. 652–54; Arthur J. Ammann et al., "Acquired Immunodeficiency in an Infant: Possible Transmission by Means of Blood Products," *Lancet* (1983-i), pp. 956–58; and telephone interview with Herbert Perkins, medical director, Irwin Memorial Blood Bank, San Francisco, June 13, 1983.

7. Joseph A. Church et al., "IgG Subclass Deficiencies in Children with Suspected AIDS," *Lancet* (1984-i), p. 279; Randi Henderson, "Losing a Child to AIDS," *Baltimore Sun*, February 15, 1984; "Infant's Death from AIDS Tied to Transfusion," *Washington Post*, September 1, 1983; Sandy Rovner, "Healthtalk: AIDS and Blood," *Washington Post*, February 3, 1984; Joan Sweeney, "Doctor Suspects AIDS Killed Infants," *Los Angeles Times*, July 27, 1983; Lois Timnick, "The Heartbreak of AIDS: A Family Copes," *Los Angeles Times*, January 13, 1984; and statement of Helen G. Kushnick for the Samuel Jared Kushnick Foundation, before a hearing of the Subcommittee on Labor, Health and Human Services, Education and Related Agencies, of the Committee on Appropriations, April 11, 1984.

8. Lois Timnick, "L.A. AIDS Case Provides Insight to Medical Sleuths," *Los Angeles Times*, March 18, 1984.

9. James W. Curran et al., "Acquired Immunodeficiency Syndrome (AIDS) Associated with Transfusions," *New England Journal of Medicine*, vol. 310 (1984), pp. 69–75; and S. C. Deresinski et al., "AIDS Transmission via Transfusion Therapy," *Lancet* (1984-i), p. 102.

10. Marilyn Chase, " 'Gift of Life' May Be Also an Agent of Death in Some AIDS Cases," *Wall Street Journal*, March 12, 1984; and CDC, "Update: AIDS—United States."

11. Marilyn Chase, "U.S. Scientists Say They've Found a Virus That Causes AIDS, but a Cure Is Years Off," *Wall Street Journal*, April 24, 1984; P. M. Feorino et al., "Lymphadenopathy Associated Virus Infection of a Blood Donor–Recipient Pair with Acquired Immunodeficiency Syndrome," *Science*, vol. 225 (1984), pp. 69–72; Robert C. Gallo et al., "Frequent Detection and Isolation of Cytopathic Retroviruses (HTLV-III) from Patients with AIDS and at Risk for AIDS," *Science*, vol. 224 (1984), pp. 500–502; Jean L. Marx, "Strong New Candidate for AIDS Agent," *Science*, vol. 224 (1984), pp. 475–77; Marilyn Chase, "The Race to Develop Vaccine against AIDS Mobilizes Researchers," *Wall Street Journal*, September 4, 1984; and Harry Nelson, "Despite Gains on AIDS, Vaccine Believed Distant," *Los Angeles Times*, September 11, 1984.

12. U.S. Public Health Service, Centers for Disease Control, "Prevention of Acquired Immune Deficiency Syndrome (AIDS): Report of Inter-Agency Recommendations," *Morbidity and Mortality Weekly Report*, vol. 32 (1983), pp. 101–3.

13. National Hemophilia Foundation, Medical and Scientific Advisory Council, *Rec-*

ommendations to Prevent AIDS in Patients with Hemophilia (New York, 1983).

14. Alpha Therapeutic Corporation, *Press Information: Alpha Therapeutic Acts to Protect Hemophiliacs from AIDS Epidemic*, January 12, 1983; Chase, " 'Gift of Life' May Be Agent of Death"; David J. Gury, "AIDS and the Paid Donor," *Lancet* (1983-II), p. 575; and idem, "AIDS Report" (Los Angeles: Alpha Therapeutic Corporation, internal memorandum, May 31, 1983).

15. American Blood Resources Association, *ABRA Recommendations on AIDS and Plasma Donor Deferral* (Annapolis, Md., January 28, 1983).

16. U.S. Food and Drug Administration, National Center for Drugs and Biologics, *Recommendations to Decrease the Risk of Transmitting Acquired Immune Deficiency Syndrome (AIDS) from Plasma Donors*, Memorandum from John C. Petricciani, director, to all establishments collecting source plasma (human) (Bethesda, Md., March 24, 1983).

17. "Blood Product Recalled over AIDS Donor," *Washington Post*, August 30, 1983; and Ronald Sullivan, "Blood Plasma Is Withdrawn over Link to AIDS," *New York Times*, November 2, 1983.

18. William A. Check, "Preventing AIDS Transmission: Should Blood Donors Be Screened?" *Journal of the American Medical Association*, vol. 249 (1983), pp. 567–70.

19. American Association of Blood Banks, American Red Cross, and Council of Community Blood Centers, *Joint Statement on Acquired Immune Deficiency Syndrome (AIDS) Related to Transfusion* (January 13, 1983); and idem, *Joint Statement on Prevention of Acquired Immune Deficiency Syndrome Related to Transfusion* (March 7, 1983).

20. U.S. Food and Drug Administration, National Center for Drugs and Biologics, *Recommendations to Decrease the Risk of Transmitting Acquired Immune Deficiency Syndrome (AIDS) from Blood Donors*, Memorandum from John C. Petricciani, director, to all establishments collecting human blood for transfusion (Bethesda, Md., March 24, 1983); idem, *Source Material Used to Manufacture Certain Plasma Derivatives*, Memorandum from John C. Petricciani, director, to all licensed manufacturers of plasma derivatives (Bethesda, Md., March 24, 1983); American Association of Blood Banks, *Before You Donate You Should Know . . .* (Arlington, Va., n.d.), p. 1; idem, *Questions and Answers about Blood and Blood Banking*, 3d ed. (Washington, D.C.: American Association of Blood Banks, 1979), p. 13; and American Red Cross, Donor Registration Form (Form 4574, rev. April 1983).

21. American Red Cross, Donor Registration Form (Form 4574, rev. April 1983); American Red Cross, *What You Should Know about Giving Blood* (ARC 1786, rev. August 1980 and January 1984); idem, *An Important Message to All Blood Donors* (ARC 1786-A, March 1983); and idem, *AIDS: Answers to Blood Donors Questions* (Form 302, August 1983).

22. Edward O. Carr, president, American Association of Blood Banks, *Standard Operating Procedures for Acquired Immune Deficiency Syndrome (AIDS)*, Memorandum to AABB institutional and associate institutional members (Arlington, Va.: AABB National Office, April 4, 1983); American Association of Blood Banks, *An Important Message to All Blood Donors* (Arlington, Va.: AABB National Office, April 4, 1983).

23. Alfred J. Katz, executive director, American Red Cross Blood Services, *AIDS Information*, Memorandum to executive heads, directors, medical scientific directors (Washington, D.C.: Blood Services Letter No. 83-12, January 26, 1983), Attachment I, *Recommendations for Blood Donor Policies with Reference to Acquired Immune Deficiency Syndrome (AIDS)*, pp. 1–2; AABB, ANRC, and CCBC, *Joint Statement on AIDS Related to Transfusion*, p. 1; and American Red Cross, "News Release: Red Cross Responds to Concern about AIDS" (Washington, D.C., January 14, 1983), pp. 1, 3.

24. Paul R. Thompson, medical director, American Red Cross Blood Services, Los Angeles–Orange Counties Region, "Instructions for Nurses Regarding Acquired Immune Deficiency Syndrome," Memorandum to nursing staff (Los Angeles, February 14, 1983); idem, "Additional Guidelines Regarding AIDS," Memorandum to all staff nurses (Los Angeles, July 27, 1983); and Carroll L. Spurling, executive director, American Red Cross Blood Services, Los Angeles–Orange Counties Region, "Acquired Im-

mune-Deficiency Syndrome (AIDS) and Blood Transfusion," Memorandum for directors of hospital blood banks and transfusion services, Los Angeles and Orange counties (Los Angeles, February 10, 1983). See also "Donors Who Lie Deserve the Blame," *USA Today*, March 23, 1984; and Robert Cooke, "AIDS Disorder Scares Off Blood Donors and Recipients," *Boston Globe*, July 29, 1983.

25. Ronald W. Powell, "AIDS Diagnosed in Blood Donor to Fourteen People," *Sacramento Bee*, March 22, 1984; and Fran Smith, "AIDS Patient Donates Blood Thirteen Times," *Santa Ana Register*, April 16, 1984.

26. Joseph Bove, "Bee Stings Kill More Than Tainted Blood," *USA Today*, March 23, 1984.

27. Chase, " 'Gift of Life' May Be Agent of Death."

28. Rovner, "Healthtalk: AIDS and Blood."

29. Virginia M. Apuzzo, "Don't Blame Donors; Screen Blood Instead," *USA Today*, March 23, 1984.

30. Chase, " 'Gift of Life' May Be Agent of Death"; American Association of Physicians for Human Rights, *The A.A.P.H.R. Statement on A.I.D.S. and Healthful Gay Male Sexual Activity: AIDS and Blood Donation* (San Francisco, n.d.); U.S. Public Health Service, *Facts about AIDS* (Washington, D.C., April 1984); and Ann Hoppe, deputy director, Blood Division, Office of Biologics, Food and Drug Administration, U.S. Department of Health and Human Services, interview by telephone, Bethesda, Maryland, April 13, 1984.

31. AABB, ANRC, and CCBC, *Joint Statement on AIDS Related to Transfusion* p. 2.

32. Harvey M. Sapolsky and Stan N. Finkelstein, "Blood Policy Revisited—A New Look at 'The Gift Relationship,'" *Public Interest*, no. 46 (1977), pp. 18–19.

33. Spurling, "The Safety of Our Blood Supply: Understanding of Blood Banking Can Mitigate Concerns about AIDS"; and "As AIDS Scare Hits Nation's Blood Supply —," *U.S. News and World Report*, July 25, 1983, p. 72.

34. Paul Jacobs, "U.S. Seeks to Halt Spread of New Disease," *Los Angeles Times*, March 4, 1983.

35. Katz, *AIDS Information* (Blood Services Letter No. 83-12), Attachment III, *Cryoprecipitated AHF and AHF Concentrates*, p. 2.

36. Chase, " 'Gift of Life' May Be Agent of Death."

37. Henderson, "Losing a Child to AIDS."

38. Joseph R. Bove, "Transfusion-Associated AIDS—A Cause for Concern," *New England Journal of Medicine*, vol. 310 (1984), pp. 115–16.

39. Joseph Bove, "Bee Stings Kill More Than Tainted Blood."

40. Chase, " 'Gift of Life' May Be Agent of Death"; and Alfred J. Katz, "Blood's Value Far Exceeds Risks," *USA Today*, March 23, 1984.

41. "As AIDS Scare Hits Nation's Blood Supply—," p. 72.

42. Bruce A. Lenes, "Designated Donations and AIDS," *CCBC Newsletter*, June 10, 1983.

43. Michael Rock, legislative assistant to Representative Shuster, interview by telephone, Washington, D.C., April 17, 1984; and John D. Milam, president, American Association of Blood Banks, letter to Representative Shuster, Arlington, Va., January 25, 1984.

44. American Association of Blood Banks, American Red Cross, and Council of Community Blood Centers, *Joint Statement on Directed Donations and AIDS*, June 22, 1983.

45. "Blood Bank Opens AIDS-Risk Hotline," *Santa Ana Register*, January 10, 1984; and Linda H. Oberman, "Red Cross to Open AIDS Phone Line," *Charleston Post-Courier*, January 30, 1984.

46. American Blood Commission, *Acquired Immune Deficiency Syndrome (AIDS) and*

Safety of Blood Donation and Blood Transfusion (January 9, 1984), p. 2.

47.　Ibid.

48.　Samir K. Ballas et al., "Designated Blood Donations," *New England Journal of Medicine*, vol. 310 (1984), pp. 124–25, excerpted by permission of the *New England Journal of Medicine*. See also David Holley, "Many Fearful of Risks in Blood Transfusion," *Los Angeles Times*, December 27, 1983; and Rovner, "Healthtalk: AIDS and Blood."

49.　AABB, ANRC, and CCBC, *Joint Statement on Directed Donations and AIDS*.

50.　"As AIDS Scare Hits Nation's Blood Supply—," p. 72.

51.　American Association of Blood Banks, "News Release: Blood Banking Organizations Reaffirm Directed Donation Recommendations," Arlington, Va., September 2, 1983, p. 2.

52.　Miller, *A Message about AIDS and Transfusion*, p. 2.

53.　"AIDS Fear Threatens Blood Services," *American Medical News*, July 15, 1983.

54.　"Irwin Initiates Directed Donation Program," *AABB News Briefs*, July 1984, pp. 1, 4.

6
New Policy Approaches

Indiscriminate solicitation, because the donor pool is so large, yields too much tainted blood.

REUBEN A. KESSEL[1]

This country's arrangements for collecting whole blood and plasma have evolved over the past decade in the direction that Richard Titmuss would have wanted. Cash blood is gone. Nonprofit organizations control blood collection in regional enclaves. One national collecting organization, incorporated by Congress, has enormous influence.

These arrangements appeared at the time to be a reasonable solution to the problems of the 1970s, but now they are the problem itself. One of the National Blood Policy's goals is *"Quality.* Attainment of the highest standards of blood transfusion therapy through full application of currently available scientific knowledge, as well as through advancement of the scientific base."[2] But this goal has been subverted by other policy provisions that encourage too many donors, too little quality competition, too much monopoly, and too little product liability. My proposals would make the quality of blood the paramount goal by taking advantage of two strengths of our present arrangements—a relatively competitive private sector plasma industry and the absence of a single nationwide blood service.

My approach to analyzing this group of issues comes from economics alone. Skeptics might argue that competition, liability, and blood quality are too different to be studied with the lens of a single discipline, but I think a single perspective is in fact a strength. Taking a different disciplinary perspective on each issue requires the analysis to change when the issue changes. Choosing a less eclectic but intellectually unified approach reveals links between issues that might not otherwise have been seen. It also reveals the explanatory power of a coherent and consistent perspective, especially for issues that were thought to be outside the normal realm of economics.

Fewer Donors

In 1981 some 8 million blood donors in the United States gave an average of 1.5 times each. Precise data are difficult to assemble, of course, because blood is not collected through registries. People move, change their names, and sometimes cannot recall how often they have donated. Blood collectors vary in the details of their record keeping. Attitudes of donors have been surveyed, but usually not carefully enough to draw strong conclusions. Nevertheless, the various estimates tend to converge. The American National Red Cross reported that the donation rate per individual for forty-three of its fifty-seven regions in 1982–1983 was 1.6 units. In 1984 it said that the "frequency of donation averages somewhere between 1.3 and 1.6 times per year, with 1.5 being the most frequently used point estimate, and with the range among donors being much larger."[3] The average for ANRC blood services in the Los Angeles and Orange counties region in 1983 was 1.495 donations (see table 1). Only about 60 percent of the region's donors in the previous two years also gave in 1983. Although blood collectors realize that repeat donors are usually more desirable, too few respond often enough to solicitation appeals to avoid adding many new donors to the pool each year, often at random.

A donor pool of this nature spread hepatitis to between 7 and 12.7 percent of transfusion patients in the mid- and late 1970s. Many of these people did not realize that they had been ill. Some of them spread the disease to family and friends by nontransfusion routes and to strangers by donating blood. Because of the variety of hepatitis agents, some patients could suffer additional attacks if they were transfused again. Posttransfusion hepatitis remains a major public health problem, despite the American Blood Commission's claim that its risk is "minimal today." The risk would be minimal in fact only if present procedures for screening blood and plasma suppliers could not be improved.

Some improvements would be relatively easy. Women are less likely than men to be carriers of either hepatitis or AIDS. Both table 1 and the survey of three cities by Drake, Finkelstein, and Sapolsky in 1976 suggest that about twice as many men as women donate blood. Titmuss summarized several surveys of noncash donors in the United States during the 1960s. Between 78 and 94 percent were men, in an era when cash and noncash collection centers were usually located downtown and more women worked at home.[4] That men donors now outnumber women by only two to one is an improvement.

Men still predominate for several reasons. Some women cannot donate because of health criteria. Blood collectors solicit at workplaces, where employees may get released time to donate and where more men than women are often employed. Providing transport to and from donor centers could attract women who meet health criteria but work at home. Giving them travel vouchers or cash instead might be simpler.

Current policies often exclude donors over sixty-five without a physician's written authorization. This policy is not unreasonable, but it arbitrarily removes a growing segment of society from the donor pool. Perhaps older donors should donate only half the usual volume of blood. Perhaps more of them would donate if blood collectors provided standard forms for physicians' consents, transportation between homes and doctor's offices to obtain consents, and transportation between homes and donor centers. Giving them travel vouchers or cash instead might also be simpler.

Adopting registries would increase the number of *safe and repeat* donors. The distinction between cash and noncash blood is less important than the distinction between blood collected extensively from random donors and blood collected from registered persons only. Revising the National Blood Policy to encourage registries, cash or noncash, would also eliminate an internal inconsistency.

> Although this policy seeks an end to the practice of purchasing whole blood and blood components from donors, it is not intended to preclude special arrangements where very rare blood or blood components are needed on an individual basis and can be obtained only by special consideration for unique donors who have been carefully evaluated.[5]

Why should some persons with rare blood types receive cash but persons in the general public be denigrated when they sell blood?

Cash registries have two advantages: the number of potential suppliers increases, and buyers can get more blood from low-risk groups by raising prices selectively. Some commercial fractionators, for example, now make products from the plasma of women only. In contrast, the AIDS experience showed that nonprofit and quasi-governmental collectors will be under pressure not to "discriminate" even if patients' health is jeopardized. Some communities may respond better to noncash solicitation. But the opposite may be true elsewhere, and we should be pragmatic about the difference. Blood should be bought if buying it can reduce disease.

Experience would show whether total costs were less with registries or with the present blood-collection system. Total costs exceed the budgeted expenses of soliciting, collecting, processing, distributing, and transfusing blood. They should include the disease costs to insurers and taxpayers, the anguish and opportunity costs to patients, and the opportunity costs to physicians, scholars, and public health authorities. Collecting blood indiscriminately from volunteers is not cheap to society if it causes unnecessary morbidity and mortality. I would expect registries to reduce total costs, but whether they would do so can be investigated. Registries should not again be rejected out of hand as HEW did a decade ago.

Some might expect registries to increase the expense of recruiting donors (as opposed to increasing total social costs), but it is unclear without further study whether they would do so. The rules of cost accounting employed by nonprofit collectors may not reflect all the resources they use. In any event, blood collectors could increase "processing" fees if registries raised their operating expenses. Probably many patients would be willing to spend a few more dollars on each transfusion if they expected it to yield higher-quality blood.

More Quality Competition

In their book *The American Blood Supply*, written before the AIDS problem, Drake, Finkelstein, and Sapolsky argued that blood is of high quality now that it is almost entirely noncash, that blood bankers run the system efficiently, and that any disease spread by the blood supply is "largely unavoidable."[6] Apparently the authors believed that the nonprofit collectors knew what quality of blood Americans wanted and could provide it. Without competition, however, it was difficult for the authors or anyone else to know how good a job the collectors were doing.

Significant, stable rates of hepatitis have been tolerated for almost a decade by every sector of the business—patients, physicians, for-profit plasma collectors, and nonprofit blood bankers. Before AIDS, both blood and plasma collectors accepted blood from groups known to be at high risk for hepatitis. Until 1983 persons were rejected only if routine blood tests for HBsAg were positive or their health histories were adverse, even though neither procedure minimized the risk of non-A, non-B carriers. For-profit and nonprofit collectors solicited so indiscriminately that high disease rates were inevitable.

Information about hepatitis was initially slow to spread, partly because the disease is so insidious. Adjustment to new knowledge was slower than necessary, as Kessel argued, because both groups of collectors were exempted from strict liability in tort. Competitive pressures to improve screening were relatively weak for the nonprofit organizations because the National Blood Policy discouraged competition. They were weak for the for-profit firms because they knew how little screening the nonprofit collectors did.

Probably many more people died in 1983 of transfusion hepatitis than of transfusion AIDS, but AIDS quickly produced fear and turmoil among blood and plasma collectors. Both groups improved screening, but the nonprofit collectors faced fewer competitors thanks to the National Blood Policy. This weakened their incentives to worry about what consumers wanted. The three major nonprofit collectors also made policy jointly on some issues where their interests diverged from those of consumers. In 1983 Edward O. Carr, president of the American Association of Blood Banks, approved of these agreements because they "increased cooperation between the major blood collecting organizations. Much good has come from this, and just in time. Our collective ability to respond to the AIDS crisis is an outstanding example of intraorganizational cooperation [within the American Blood Commission]."[7] But competition might have led to greater improvement in donor screening.

Competition caused a superior response, from the perspective of consumers, among the for-profit organizations. Each firm faced for-profit and nonprofit rivals. Each also faced potential competition from new manufacturers that could screen donors even more selectively. Their performance in 1983 was scarcely perfect, but it should alleviate old fears that for-profit collectors do a social disservice just by purchasing plasma or blood.

The response of the for-profit industry to AIDS contrasts with its response to hepatitis a decade earlier. Some of its customers in the 1970s developed immunity from hepatitis owing to multiple transfusions before HBsAg screening became widespread. But children and adults who had received few transfusions remained at risk, and some died.[8] AIDS was different because victims did not develop immunity from further attacks. Death from AIDS was also more gruesome, inevitable, and newsworthy.

Some patients thought that directed donations would yield higher-quality blood and were worth the extra costs of finding donors and perhaps paying higher hospital charges. It is likely that more patients would have attempted these procedures in 1983 if the nonprofit blood collectors had not jointly opposed them. A few AABB members and university medical centers allowed them, but not enough to change the joint policy.

More competition among for-profit and nonprofit collectors of whole blood would indicate what quality patients preferred and whether that quality required better screening than the nonprofit collectors have provided. AIDS is so dangerous that I would expect only one quality of blood to survive. I would expect that quality to reflect the screening standards employed by the for-profit collectors rather than by the nonprofit collectors in 1983 if these were the only two choices. I would also expect to find more registries in a competitive regime or with a rule of strict product liability in tort.

The National Blood Policy should be amended to encourage for-profit firms to provide blood and blood components of any kind in addition to plasma products. It should also encourage directed donations where patients and physicians demand them.

Less Monopoly

Drake, Finkelstein, and Sapolsky argued in 1982 that increased cartelization of blood banking in most urban regions, owing to the National Blood Policy and the ABC's regionalization program, required "effective public oversight mechanisms."[9] More competition would be the most effective oversight mechanism.

I have described certain steps that the ANRC took in its failed attempt to become a government-sanctioned monopolist of civilian blood supplies, even though blood activities were not included in its federal incorporation. The controversy over cash blood in the 1970s was caused not only by the ANRC's desire to protect the public but, as Gordon Tullock suggested, by its desire for less competition from for-profit organizations. Later it was willing to provoke a public quarrel with its main nonprofit rival by withdrawing from the National Clearinghouse. It considered building a fractionation plant jointly with a commercial rival to strengthen its position in the plasma market. It joined with other nonprofit collectors to oppose directed donations.

One cannot blame the ANRC for wanting less competition; most organizations would seize the same opportunity if it were available. The key question is whether a nationwide blood monopoly or even the regional monopolies and cartels we now have are in the public interest. Having a strong coordinating organization in each region that can quickly respond to emergencies is undoubtedly an advantage. The public may lose some of this advantage in the communications industry, for example, owing to the breakup of the Bell system. But a more competitive communications industry has many other advantages that are more than offsetting. This is also likely to be true for blood.

More competition is not likely to come from the nonprofit organizations. The AABB and the Council of Community Blood Centers opposed the ANRC's ambition for a nationwide system. But all three opposed cash blood and jointly developed other policies that reduced competition among them. The National Blood Policy should encourage competition among nonprofit collectors as well as between nonprofit and for-profit collectors. Its policy of regionalization should be reversed, and the ABC's regional agreements should be reviewed for antitrust content by the U.S. Department of Justice.

More Liability

By the 1970s most states had given exemptions to blood banks and manufacturers of blood products from the doctrine of strict liability in tort. To obtain damages for a posttransfusion disease, the plaintiff had to prove that blood or blood products were collected, manufactured, or handled negligently. Since proving negligence was more difficult than proving that a posttransfusion disease had occurred, these statutes drastically reduced the value of damages won in products liability lawsuits.

These exemptions varied in statutory and case law. Most frequently blood and blood derivatives were declared to be "services" rather than "products" even if they were manufactured and sold at market prices by for-profit firms. In some states blood banks and manufacturers were exempted from an obligation to offer implied warranties in contract. The presence of HBsAg was not viewed as a medicinal adulteration or filth. Blood banks could use the defenses that they had screened donors and tested blood in the laboratory according to standards used customarily throughout the trade or that they had complied with FDA regulations. In some wrongful death cases the risks of transfusion were believed to be outweighed by the risks to life without transfusion. Registries were not contemplated in the cases that I examined.[10]

A 1981 case suggests that these defenses are not impregnable, however. The Supreme Court of Louisiana held that the standard for an "unreasonably dangerous" product or service should not be based on either the standard blood-banking practices for screening donors or the risks of transfusing versus not transfusing. " 'Unreasonably dangerous' means simply that the article which injured the plaintiff was dangerous to an extent beyond that which would be contemplated by an ordinary consumer."[11] This decision, which reversed the holding of a lower court in favor of the defendant blood bank, might affect for-profit and nonprofit collectors.[12]

Kessel argued that exemption of blood banks from strict liability in tort was anticonsumer legislation obtained through the efforts of a coalition of medical societies, hospitals, and blood banks (nonprofit and for-profit). Its purpose was to shift the costs of hepatitis to patients. He also argued that the absence of strict liability for blood was anomalous in a country where producers of lawn mowers, ladders, soft-drink bottles, medicines, automobiles, and many other hazardous consumer goods were held accountable for injuries in which their products were implicated. Imposing strict liability on blood banks made sense because patients (especially in emergencies) had less information on high-risk donors than collectors had. Blood banks could mitigate damages at a lower cost than patients.[13]

Making blood and plasma collectors strictly liable in tort for post-transfusion disease would strengthen their incentives to screen donors more carefully.[14] It might also be the most important incentive for them to adopt registries, which would lower premiums for malpractice insurance or the costs of self-insurance.

The National Blood Policy should encourage strict liability in tort, but with a caveat about the possibility of joint causation. In the Louisiana case, a woman contracted hepatitis B in 1973 one month after surgery and transfusion. The two units transfused were HBsAg-negative by the best but only partially effective testing procedures at the time. Two months after the transfusion, the blood of one of her suppliers was HBsAg-positive. The victim's sister had contracted hepatitis B a year earlier, although she was asymptomatic at the time of surgery. The court concluded that the timing of the disease suggested that the transfusion rather than the sister was at fault. The trial included testimony of expert witnesses who established "that Type B hepatitis is generally transmitted parenterally, most commonly by a transfusion of hepatitis-infected blood."[15] By the late 1970s, however, it was known that hepatitis B was transmitted by household contacts as well as by transfusion. Knowing this earlier might have affected the court's decision.

Joint causation may be relevant in some cases of transfusion AIDS, but lawsuits were filed in 1984 in California and New York by AIDS victims (or their relatives) where no other risk factor was believed to be present. The consumer of a plasma product sued the manufacturer for a failure to screen donors and test for filth sufficiently. Others sued hospitals or blood banks for negligence, attempting to overturn statutes (found in forty-five states) making blood a service rather than a product. One plaintiff argued that the New York statute, enacted in response to the posttransfusion hepatitis problem, should not limit liability for AIDS because AIDS is almost always lethal. It was reported in the *Wall Street Journal* in August 1984 that opposition to using the T-cell and hepatitis core antibody tests by manufacturers, blood banks, and hospitals was beginning to erode.[16]

A rule of strict liability in tort would quickly cause far-reaching changes in blood industry practices. It would be costly and time-consuming to achieve, however, state by state through legislation, and the outcomes of the AIDS wrongful death cases are difficult to predict. Some of the same benefits would occur gradually if the National Blood Policy encouraged blood-banking competition. Patients and physicians would eventually learn through literature, the media, and word of mouth which organizations offered safer blood, just as they now learn about the quality of hospitals, drugs, and medical procedures. They would demand more blood from collectors that screen donors more carefully. These organizations would set the quality standard. Competition would challenge the for-profit collectors to show that they can offer high-quality blood. It would challenge the nonprofit collectors to show that they can offer high-quality blood without governmental favoritism.

Over a decade ago the National Blood Policy was established on the premise that competition was bad. But there is no more reason to exclude commercial firms from making a profit in the blood business than to exclude the American National Red Cross from earning more revenues than costs in the plasma business. If competition between nonprofit and for-profit collectors helps consumers, the reverse is also true. Too little competition has made us rely on too many donors, too little quality competition, too much monopoly, and too little liability of collectors for the quality of their blood and plasma products. These defects were important enough when the main disease conveyed by transfusion was hepatitis, but they are even more so with AIDS. More competition in blood banking will ameliorate each of the institutional defects that keep American public health lower than it needs to be.

Notes

1. Reuben A. Kessel, "Transfused Blood, Serum Hepatitis, and the Coase Theorem," *Journal of Law and Economics*, vol. 17 (1974), p. 282.

2. U.S. Department of Health, Education, and Welfare, Office of the Secretary, "National Blood Policy: Proposed Implementation Plan; Requests for Comments," *Federal Register*, vol. 39 (1974), p. 9329.

3. Paul D. Cumming, manager, planning, marketing, and operations research, American Red Cross, Washington, D.C., to Ross D. Eckert, Claremont, July 26, 1984, personal files of Ross D. Eckert, Claremont, California; American Red Cross, Blood Services, *Viewpoints, 1982–83*, p. 10; and Alvin W. Drake, Stan N. Finkelstein, and Harvey M. Sapolsky, *The American Blood Supply* (Cambridge, Mass., and London: MIT Press, 1982), p. 5.

4. Richard M. Titmuss, *The Gift Relationship: From Human Blood to Social Policy* (New York: Vintage Books, 1972), chap. 6.

5. HEW, "National Blood Policy: Proposed Implementation Plan," p. 9329.

6. Drake et al., p. 126.

7. Edward O. Carr, "Progress Made in Implementing the National Blood Policy:

A Ten Year Retrospective and Recommendations for the Future," paper delivered to a meeting of the American Blood Commission, August 3, 1983.

8. Fogo v. Cutter Laboratories, Inc., 68 C.A. 3d 744 (1977).

9. Drake et al., pp. 141–42.

10. Hutchins v. Blood Services of Montana, 506 P. 2d 449 (1973); Juneau v. Interstate Blood Bank, Inc. of Louisiana, 1333 So. 2d 354 (1976); Adams v. New Orleans Blood-Bank, Inc., 343 So. 2d 363 (1977); Fogo v. Cutter Laboratories; Moore v. Underwood Memorial Hospital, 371 A. 2d 105 (1977); Gilmore v. St. Anthony Hospital, 598 P. 2d 1200 (1979). See also Marc A. Franklin, "Tort Liability for Hepatitis: An Analysis and a Proposal," *Stanford Law Review*, vol. 24 (1972), pp. 474–79.

11. DeBattista v. Argonaut-Southwest Insurance Co., 403 So. 2d 26, at 30 (1981).

12. These cases are surveyed in Richard Landfield, "Some Thoughts about AIDS, Blood Products, and Products Liability Laws," *Plasma Quarterly*, vol. 5 (Fall 1983), p. 70.

13. Kessel, pp. 281–82.

14. Ibid., pp. 275–89.

15. Debattista v. Argonaut-Southwest Insurance Co., p. 29.

16. Marilyn Chase, "AIDS Suits Focus on Blood Safeguards," *Wall Street Journal*, August 20, 1984; and "The State," *Los Angeles Times*, September 7, 1984.

The Case for
National Blood Policy
Edward L. Wallace

Acknowledgments

When I was first approached to write this paper, it was with the understanding that it would serve as a companion to the one by Ross Eckert, presenting an alternative view. As my paper progressed, however, it became apparent that a simple response to Eckert's paper would be too narrow and too technical to be of interest to the general reader. A broader approach was needed to provide the background required to understand the complex issues faced by the blood services in the 1970s and 1980s and to judge the propriety of actions taken by public officials and private managers to resolve them. It was the realization of this that led to this expanded work.

I was assisted in producing the work by several persons whose efforts I very much appreciate. I am especially grateful to Kristina Baum of the American Red Cross who secured for me many of the copies of the earlier references as well as background materials. Dr. Julian Schorr of the American Red Cross read the entire manuscript and made a number of useful suggestions. In particular, I would like to thank Dr. Paul Cumming of the American Red Cross with whom I have had a long and productive relationship both as a friend and research colleague. Dr. Cumming's earlier work, *National Blood Policy and the American Blood Commission*, for which I served in an advisory role, formed the basis for much of my knowledge of events that transpired in blood services in the 1970s. Dr. Cumming served as a valuable critic and commentator on my paper.

My wife, Mary Ann Wallace, typed and edited the final manuscript and made several improvements in the presentation. Without her assistance and frequent encouragement the project would have moved much more slowly than it did.

The work is not a response by the American Red Cross. It represents my assessment of events that occurred in blood services during the last fifteen years and of the outlook for the future. Whatever errors of fact or judgment it may contain are attributable only to me.

1
Introduction

The early 1970s were a chaotic time in blood services: demands on the system outstripped its ability to respond; blood and blood products were wasted at unreasonable rates; access of those in need was often severely restricted; and the quality of blood products was suspect because of hepatitis contamination. All these problems interacted with one another, forming a complex set of issues that the blood services community found difficult to deal with. The proposed solution was the National Blood Policy—a comprehensive set of guidelines to transform the organization and operation of the nation's blood services, formulated by public officials with the advice and assistance of private blood service managers.

The history of blood services in the United States in the 1970s is the history of the National Blood Policy, a unique combination of federal initiative and policy making with private sector cooperation and implementation. It is perhaps the best example of how government effort joined to private sector competence can bring about a major transformation in health care.

Included in the transformation were the events discussed in Ross Eckert's work. The transformation, however, was broader than simply a reduction in transfusion-related disease or enhancement of the role of nonprofit organizations, including the American Red Cross, in blood services. It also involved major increases in the supply and array of available blood products and services, substantial changes in methods of managing and distributing supply, and a revision of attitudes toward access to the supply and responsibility for its replenishment. All of these were closely related to one another and to the issue of quality, which is the major focus of Eckert's work.

Chapter 1 offers a comprehensive overview of the issues facing the blood services in the early 1970s: events leading up to the issuance of the National Blood Policy, actions taken by public officials and private organizations to implement the policy, and changes that occurred in the blood services system as a result of these efforts. The chapter concludes with a survey of recent developments in blood services and the problems that face the industry in the 1980s.

Chapter 2 focuses on the issue of blood quality—past and present—and the problems that would attend reentry of commercial blood services and the paid donor into the blood products sector of the industry. It expands upon the background that is presented in Eckert's work and provides a different assessment of past events and statistics. It also includes a comprehensive assessment of the risks to patients of contracting AIDS or non-A, non-B hepatitis as a result of a transfusion. The chapter concludes with a set of public policy recommendations that are different from those of Eckert.

Chapter 3 discusses the growth of regionalism in blood services and the conflicting philosophies of individual and community responsibility for ensuring replacement of the transfused blood supply. The principal theme of the chapter is how this conflict in philosophy underlies and explains most of the past and present differences between the American Red Cross and the American Association of Blood Banks. The work concludes with a brief assessment of the problems facing blood services in the 1980s and some recommendations about how the system might deal with these problems more effectively.

2

The Blood Services System in the 1970s and 1980s

The 1970s were a time of great change in the blood services system of the United States. Major transformations took place in the organization and functioning of the whole blood and blood components sectors. The blood derivatives sector also changed appreciably in both concentration and growth. Most of the events and issues of concern to Ross Eckert occurred and were decided during this period. Only acquired immune deficiency syndrome (AIDS) is an issue new to the 1980s.

To persons outside the blood services system, the great debates over blood policy in the United States began in 1971 with American publication of *The Gift Relationship*, by the Englishman Richard Titmuss.[1] Titmuss's work, which had an energizing effect on public opinion about blood quality and blood donation as a social act, was in part an outgrowth of studies and debates among American blood services professionals during the 1960s.[2] By his skillful use of available evidence on poor blood quality and his considerable powers of argument and persuasion about the ethical aspects of voluntary blood donation, Titmuss focused public and governmental attention on two of a number of blood policy issues then being debated by blood services professionals. He made both the public and the politicians aware of the hepatitis risk associated with blood transfusion, but in doing so he narrowed the area of public debate on blood policy to the issues of quality and commercialism. The results were both beneficial and detrimental to the interests of blood services: beneficial in that increased public attention and the threat of government intervention forced the contending interests in the blood services system and the government to begin a loosely coordinated effort to confront the issues, detrimental in that heightened public attention brought pressure to do something about the quality of blood and blood donation and shunted aside other important issues.

Blood Issues in 1971

At the time Titmuss's book was published, the blood services system faced a number of policy issues. Some were the result of changing attitudes toward health care stemming from major changes in government and public involvement in its planning and financing. Others arose from changes in the organization and management of blood services and scientific discoveries and advances in blood therapy. Among the more important of these issues were the following:

- frequent shortages of whole blood and blood components during certain seasons of the year in many parts of the country
- "unnecessary" use of whole blood and red blood cells
- unavailability in some areas of blood components and services
- conflicts between hospital and community blood services about responsibility for meeting total community needs for blood products and services
- conflicting attitudes toward the relative merits of volunteer and paid donors
- disease transmission through transfusion of contaminated blood products
- inadequate government regulation
- high rates of outdating of whole blood and components and large numbers of units unaccounted for
- excessive use of whole blood rather than red blood cells
- conflicting attitudes toward alternative methods of organizing and conducting functions in the blood system and of governance of blood organizations
- poor internal management of many blood services organizations
- differences in access to blood resources in different organizations and parts of the country
- lack of information on the conduct of operations in all sectors of the blood system[3]

These issues fall quite readily into five general categories—supply, quality, efficiency, accessibility, and information—presaging the goals of the National Blood Policy.

Supply Issues. The frequent shortages of blood in many parts of the country during the 1960s and early 1970s had several causes. Most important was the reluctance of donors, paid as well as volunteer, to donate blood during the year-end holiday period and in the late summer, coupled with inadequate efforts by the blood services to spread recruitment and collections evenly throughout the year.[4] Given the twenty-one-day shelf life then in effect for whole blood and red blood cells and the practice of hospital blood banks and regional and community blood centers not to carry large inventories, abrupt drops in blood collections were inevitably followed by periods of shortage. During these shortages the medical directors of blood centers and blood banks were forced to ration supplies, thereby creating frequent and often severe disputes among the directors, the blood centers, and surgeons and physicians forced to postpone elective surgery and to reduce the numbers of blood units transfused to their patients. Because the medical directors of blood centers and blood banks often imposed on surgeons and physicians their judgments about the relative needs of patients for blood, there were numerous disputes and complaints of arrogance.

The supply situation was further aggravated by differences in opinion between blood service medical directors and practicing physicians about the therapeutic justification for one-unit transfusions of whole blood or red cells to patients with slight anemias, and so on.[5] Hematologists and blood bank authorities opposed such transfusions because of presumed waste of the scarce resource and the risks of disease transmission from transfusion. Many practicing physicians, however, favored one-unit transfusions as a way of "perking-up" their patients.

Of greater importance was the reluctance of many physicians and some blood service medical directors to transfuse red cells rather than whole blood. In the early 1970s red cell component therapy was relatively new. It was not immediately accepted by surgeons and physicians even though it had the support of medical authority and the obvious benefit of maximizing the useful cellular components of whole blood. Separating red cells from plasma dramatically improved the total component supply. It also made therapy more effective by infusing only the blood component required by the patient. The technique made it possible to meet the needs of patients for improved oxygen transport and at the same time to provide a much larger pool of recovered plasma as raw material for the production of blood derivatives. This new source of plasma was needed by the blood derivatives industry, which was buying substantial amounts of plasma from third world countries. Transfusion of red cells rather than whole blood also offered a ready source of other cellular components, notably platelets and fresh plasma, which were just beginning to be widely used in medical practice.

Another problem was the unavailability in many parts of the country, particularly in rural and some large urban areas, of blood services able to provide the full array of products and services needed by the hospitals in those areas.[6] The main reason for this was excessive

91

fragmentation of competing sources, so that no one source or group of sources was able or willing to be responsible for the total area supply. This problem was further complicated in certain large urban areas by the difficulties of collecting sufficient amounts of blood from a donor population to which access was difficult and by the preference of many blood suppliers for providing only whole blood, not the less profitable and more difficult to produce blood components or other needed blood services.[7]

The early 1970s were also a time of frequent conflicts between hospital, commercial, and community blood banks and centers over the source of donated blood. Of special interest was the argument between the advocates (mostly community blood centers and some hospital blood bank directors) of an all-volunteer donor pool, and the advocates (mostly hospital blood banks and commercial blood services) of continued use of paid donors where necessary. The actual donor situation at the time was mixed: some community blood centers relied heavily on paid donors; some hospital blood banks used only volunteer donors; and many hospitals and some centers used whatever donors they could get, volunteer or paid.[8] Debate over the ethics and the economics of using paid donors for whole blood was not as intense as it became by the mid-1970s, but the nucleus of the later debate was present.

Finally, in many areas hospital blood bankers and community blood center directors had sharp differences of opinion about the responsibilities of each for ensuring a sufficient supply of whole blood, blood components, and blood services to meet the community's needs. Although many hospitals collected blood on their premises, they viewed their collections as supplementary to the blood they received from community centers. Many community blood center directors, however, saw the situation in reverse. Their organizations had frequently come into existence after the hospitals had set up their collection services. The initial purpose of many of them, especially those of the American Red Cross, was to lend their considerable abilities to helping the hospitals recruit donors. In short, they saw themselves as supplementary community blood suppliers and the hospitals as having primary responsibility for ensuring the total community supply. This was true even where the community center collected as much as 80 to 90 percent of the community's blood supply. This attitude was not uncommon among managers of American Red Cross regional blood centers, who remained oriented toward disaster relief and the other more traditional Red Cross programs.[9]

Quality. The quality of blood and blood components became an important issue in the middle to late 1960s and early 1970s. Physicians were aware that transfusion carried the risk of transmitting viral, parasitical, or bacterial disease. Tests and other methods were available to screen out parasitically and bacterially contaminated blood. Unfortunately, there was no effective means of testing donors or donated blood for the presence of viral disease, principally hepatitis. Several epidemiological studies during the 1960s associated the incidence of posttransfusion hepatitis with certain donor characteristics in an effort to identify the groups at greatest risk.[10] Most of these studies were of limited scope, but the threat involved and limited knowledge of the etiology of hepatitis left no alternative.

An added concern in the early 1970s was loose enforcement of standards of conduct for blood banks and a lack of supervision of plasma collection centers. While many blood banks were members of the American Association of Blood Banks (AABB) and adhered to its standards or to those of the American Red Cross, a number, especially the commercial blood services, did not. The commercial services were supervised primarily by state health departments, which varied widely in their standards and enforcement practices. Stories of unsanitary conditions and unreasonable collection practices in some of these organizations abounded in the media in the early 1970s, raising public and government concerns over the quality and safety of their products.[11]

Efficiency. The issue of efficiency was not as important in the late 1960s and early 1970s as it was at the end of the 1970s. Nevertheless, numerous concerns were expressed in the early 1970s about management inefficiency, especially waste of blood resources.[12] Of particular concern was the high rate of outdating of whole blood and red cells and frequent unaccounted for losses of blood units. Community blood centers did not recognize the losses as a problem because they assumed that blood units they shipped to the hospitals that were not returned were transfused. This frequently was not so, however. Hospitals did not bother to return outdated units unless the center offered some credit for their return. Since few centers did so, most hospitals disposed of units without notifying the centers.

A related issue was the question of who controlled blood resources. Most community blood centers maintained only small storage capacities, depending instead on storage of blood in the hospitals. The problem was further complicated by different charging procedures used by the various centers. Most sold the blood they collected to the hospitals; that is, they billed the hospital for the blood when it was shipped and provided credits of varying amounts when the hospitals returned blood that was not outdated. Some centers retained title to the blood in the hospitals, billing either the hospital or the

93

patient only when the blood was transfused or outdated. The control issue arose principally during periods of community shortage, when centers wished to transfer blood from one hospital to another. Under such conditions the hospitals were frequently unwilling to release blood, often claiming that they did not have it in their inventories. Even when the blood was on consignment from a center, recovery of it was very difficult because hospitals refused to release it or because the center's information about hospital inventories was incomplete and incapable of determining which hospitals were overserved.[13]

Finally, there was concern about extensive hospital collections of whole blood given its twenty-one-day shelf life. The mixture of blood types collected through replacement by medium-sized and small hospitals was frequently out of balance with the mixture required by the hospital's patients. While the amounts of these imbalances in any one hospital were generally small, in the blood system as a whole the aggregates were quite large and accounted for a substantial portion of hospital outdating. Center managements and others concerned with waste in the blood system argued that community blood centers, as suppliers to a much larger set of patients through their associated hospitals, were better able than individual collecting hospitals to match supply and demand by blood type.[14]

Access. Concern over access to blood resources took two forms in the early 1970s. The first concern was that the supply of components and derivatives available to hospitals be sufficient to meet all reasonable needs, the second that the ultimate cost to the patient be reasonable.

Many hospitals had limited access to such components as platelets, cryoprecipitate, and fresh plasma. The advent of new therapies requiring the use of components other than red cells placed demands on many hospitals and community blood centers that they were not equipped to meet. As a consequence blood therapies practiced in the major medical centers and large metropolitan hospitals far outstripped those available in most medium-sized and small hospitals.[15]

Hemophiliacs were served rather poorly at the time. Recent discoveries of cryoprecipitated AHF and development of dry concentrate AHF by the blood derivatives industry had raised the therapy expectations of hemophiliacs and their parents, whose association brought pressure on legislators and government agencies to ensure sufficient supplies of AHF and sufficient numbers of treatment centers to meet the needs of the hemophiliac population.[16]

Concerns over costs centered largely on the replacement requirement and the nonreplacement fee rather than on amounts charged for transfusion.[17] Although actual charges varied markedly among centers and hospitals for what often appeared to be unsupported and capricious reasons, it was the nonreplacement fee that captured most of the attention. The fee was an outgrowth of efforts by hospital blood banks to motivate the family and friends of blood recipients to replace the blood transfused. Because of the high rate of outdating, due largely to the short shelf life and to blood type imbalances, 2:1 or 3:1 replacement was frequently required to avoid the nonreplacement fee. The amount of the fee varied widely; in time it became an important source of funds for the hospitals and centers that used it.

The nonreplacement fee was an important tool for recruiting donors, along with efforts to persuade families and friends to donate. Blood needs of the hospitals not met by replacement were met by payments to the blood center, to paid donors—frequently the hospitals' own staffs—or to commercial sources.

The growth of community and regional blood services in the late 1950s and 1960s offered alternative means for people to assure themselves and their families of adequate blood supplies if they needed them through a variety of insurance or assurance plans. An individual and his or her family were assured of various amounts of blood by donating one or more units of blood per year to the community or regional center. Some plans used blood bank deposit credits for individuals or groups that donated, with balances maintained as in a checking account. These plans were joined with use of the nonreplacement fee by those who favored it. The result was a myriad of plans differing from community to community. Because persons who were members of a blood assurance plan in one locality often required blood therapy in another, the AABB clearinghouse came into existence, largely to handle the settlement of claims among these various plans.

In time, however, many of the regional and community blood centers began to move away from the concept of individual responsibility embodied in these plans and toward the concept of general community responsibility.[18] This difference in philosophy was just emerging in the early 1970s. Most centers and hospitals were using one or more assurance plans and charging patients for blood if they did not have assurance coverage. Titmuss's work brought the growing difference in philosophy to the forefront, and the nonreplacement fee became the symbol of the difference. From these beginnings sprang many of the later differences among the AABB, the American Red Cross, and the Council of Community Blood Centers (CCBC).

Information. Rhetoric was always in ample supply in the blood system during the early 1970s; factual information was not. The lack of information extended from scientific studies of the etiology of blood-related diseases, particularly hepatitis, to the operations of regional and community blood centers and their associated hospitals. From time to time organizations such as the American Medical Association and the AABB undertook surveys of the blood system. The surveys varied in scope, sometimes omitting information their sponsors thought to be of little interest or "too sensitive." Some surveys were limited to the members of the organizations that were only part of the blood system. Even then many members either chose not to respond or omitted responses to questions they found awkward.

In 1968 the National Heart and Lung Institute (NHLI) launched a multimillion-dollar four-year project to test the feasibility of developing computerized information systems to improve the conduct of regional and community blood service operations. The study aimed at enhancing accessibility by managing supply better and reducing waste and inefficiency. By 1972 four prototype systems had been developed and implemented with varying success. Two of the systems were accepted by the blood service managements and continued in operation after completion of the study. The other two were considered too complex and costly to warrant continuation. The study demonstrated the feasibility of such systems and their utility in blood services management. Still, they were not generally accepted by blood service managers, largely because of lack of familiarity with the equipment and concern over its costs, general reluctance to change existing systems, and an inability to use the information such systems would provide in planning and controlling blood service operations.[19]

For these reasons much of the debate over blood policy issues in the late 1960s and 1970s was based on a few limited studies or surveys or on anecdotal evidence. It was not until 1972, when the NHLI published the results of its 1971 census of blood establishments, that reasonably reliable and comprehensive data became available. Even then the data produced by the NHLI survey failed to include certain information needed to understand many of the issues. Moreover, the survey lacked information on quality and on costs and charges of blood bank and blood center operations.

The National Blood Policy, the American Blood Commission, and the Bureau of Biologics

The release of the Titmuss book in 1971 was followed by a burst of media attention focusing on hepatitis, inadequate safety regulation, the reprehensible behavior of some commercial suppliers, and wasted blood. As might be expected, action was initiated by federal and state governments. Congress was deluged with bills proposing to correct the problems, usually through increased federal regulation or direct federal involvement in the blood services system. In 1972 President Richard Nixon, as a result of the furor stirred by Titmuss and findings of the 1971 NHLI census of blood establishments, charged the Department of Health, Education, and Welfare (HEW) with responsibility for developing a safer and more efficient blood system. State health departments also began tightening their standards and enforcing them more vigorously, and state legislatures passed laws requiring that blood be labeled as drawn from paid or volunteer donors.

The situation was further complicated by concern among doctors, hospitals, and blood services over possible personal and organizational liability for posttransfusion hepatitis. The likelihood of litigation increased appreciably because of media coverage of the hepatitis issue and public perception of the association of hepatitis with the use of paid blood from commercial sources. As Kessel pointed out in his 1974 article "Transfused Blood, Serum Hepatitis, and the Coase Theorem," the specter of strict liability in tort upheld by the Illinois Supreme Court in *Cunningham* v. *MacNeal Memorial Hospital*, which found the hospital liable for damages suffered as a result of hepatitis contracted from blood transfusion in the hospital, became an additional motive for changing the system.[20]

The National Blood Policy. After President Nixon's charge to HEW, a department task force held a series of meetings at which various blood issues were debated. This effort culminated in 1973 in the issuance by HEW of the National Blood Policy. The policy and its implementation involved a mixture of pragmatic and ideological considerations. Pragmatically the department recognized the existence of two distinct sectors in the blood system—blood products and blood derivatives— and the need for different policies for each. Ideologically it developed the policy under federal guidance but determined to implement it through private means financed largely by the federal government. Ultimately, the policy's development and implementation became a social experiment to determine the extent to which a public-private form of health care planning might succeed with government support and guidance.

The policy set forth four major goals: developing an adequate blood supply, attaining the highest possible quality standards, ensuring general access to blood, and achieving greater efficiency throughout the system. These goals were to be accomplished by adherence to ten principal policies and the resolution of six critical issues. The guiding policies were to encourage and support an all-volunteer system for blood and blood components (but not blood derivatives), a system to collect and analyze information on plasmapheresis operations, systems to collect and analyze data on blood services operations, resource sharing and areawide cooperation in whole blood collection and distribution, determination of the relation between transfusion costs and charges as a means of furthering recruitment of donors, education, adherence to the highest quality standards through the use or extension of federal standards, scientific and management research on blood and blood use, and provision of insurance coverage for those in need of blood components and blood derivatives. The critical issues to be resolved included the appropriateness of the nonreplacement fee, the integration of various functions and segments of the blood banking industry, regionalism, exclusion of the commercial acquisition of whole blood and blood components, examination of the special access problems of hemophiliacs and others with extraordinary blood product needs, and the adequacy of any implementation action to meet national regional emergencies. The secretary of HEW was made responsible for implementing the policy.

The principal intent of the National Blood Policy was to foster a nationwide network of voluntary regional blood services as the primary means of implementing its other aims and policies. The American Blood Commission (ABC) was to be established to develop and implement an Integrated Regional Program. A region formed and recognized under the program was expected to[21]

- accept the responsibility for recruiting volunteer donors in the region
- include at least one facility licensed to ship blood over state lines
- provide for total blood services in its area on a schedule in keeping with the needs of the region
- have the capacity to provide expert medical consultation on hemotherapy, compatibility problems, and other blood-related problems whenever needed
- provide the range and quantity of blood components required in the region
- meet current appropriate inspection and accreditation standards
    In local areas served by several blood banks, the Integrated Regional Program will encompass all the blood services in the area, including transfusion services. Physicians and directors of the area blood banks should exert leadership in the establishment of an organization that can provide the services deemed necessary to the successful administration of an integrated program. The blood banks and the hospital services that will be served by these larger programs must

be invited to participate as they would in an area served by a single blood bank.

Each Regional Program will organize to provide quality services to the transfusion facilities in its area, recruit donors, and keep records on blood drawn and on adverse reactions. Hospital transfusion facilities receiving blood would keep inventory records, report to the Regional Program on transfusion reactions, and may be requested to draw blood if needed within the system.[22]

Much of the remaining text of the policy was devoted to a detailed discussion of the organization, operations, and governance of the proposed regions and their relationship to the ABC. Each regional system was to be the dominant blood service organization in its area, controlling all aspects of regional blood services and reporting to the ABC, which would coordinate regional operations and set policies to guide their conduct.

The announcement of the National Blood Policy was followed by actions in two spheres: in the federal agencies responsible for setting and enforcing blood establishment standards and in the private blood sectors. In 1972 responsibility for monitoring blood resources was transferred from the National Institutes of Health (NIH) to the Bureau of Biologics of the Food and Drug Administration (FDA), which was the federal agency responsible for licensing and inspecting blood establishments in the United States. In 1973 the Bureau of Biologics augmented its standards to include source plasma and required the licensing of plasmapheresis centers and products. For pragmatic reasons, as stated by Eckert, the blood derivatives sector was exempted from the all-volunteer-donor policy. Instead, the Bureau of Biologics, pressed for compliance with its standards as a means of eliminating undesirable establishments and behavior among commercial plasma collectors.

The American Blood Commission. The American Blood Commission (ABC) came into existence in 1975 as the private association designated by HEW to develop and implement the National Blood Policy.[23] Its membership and governing body comprised producers and consumers of blood services and their designated representatives. As a private voluntary association, the ABC lacks the power to enforce blood policies.

Both for-profit and nonprofit blood services joined the ABC and participated actively in its studies and deliberations along with the many consumer organizations that made up the bulk of its membership. Involvement by private producer organizations was motivated both by a desire to improve conditions in the various blood sectors and by the unstated threat of other forms of government involvement if this initiative failed. Four major initiatives were ultimately undertaken by the ABC: the achievement of standard labeling of blood products, the development of regional associations, data collection, and the development of blood policies, including resource sharing. The ABC spent over $3 million in the years that followed, over 80 percent of which came from the federal government in the form of contracts and grants.

The ABC's efforts had mixed results. Labeling was successfully standardized, regionalism and data collection were partially successful, and policy development was generally unsuccessful. The success in labeling was largely ensured by general agreement among blood services organizations that such a system was needed to further mechanization and to facilitate the exchange of products and data.

The regionalism program envisaged substantial reorganization of many whole blood and blood component services in large sections of the United States by shifting control and governance over blood collection, processing, and distribution to a single regional association. The aims of the regional associations were to improve blood services and to achieve efficiency through economies of scale. The ABC program of regionalism differed somewhat from that of the American Red Cross in that it did not require a regional association to be a single entity with full control over all aspects of regional operations; it permitted several smaller blood service organizations in a service area to coordinate their operations under the regional association while maintaining their separate identities. The effort was only partially successful: a number of regional associations, including some American Red Cross regions, applied for and received ABC recognition. In some areas where competition was intense, the formation of regional associations proved impossible because of the unwillingness of fierce competitors to cooperate with one another. In still other areas strong regional blood centers refused to apply for ABC recognition because they disagreed with one or more of the ABC's requirements, especially concerning governance.

The data collection efforts of the ABC centered on the National Blood Data Center (NBDC) and its conduct of the 1979 and 1980 national blood censuses. These censuses provided the first comprehensive overview since 1971 of the organization and operations of the whole blood and blood components sectors. Unfortunately, they did not gather data on the activities or economics of the blood derivatives sector or data on prices from community and regional blood centers. The NBDC failed to develop continuing sources of private and government funding that would have permitted it to continue operations once the two government-sponsored censuses were completed.

Policy initiatives of the ABC ranged from consideration of volunteer versus paid donors to the costing of blood products. Included were such issues as the nonreplacement fee, resource sharing, and community versus individual responsibility. If the ABC can claim any success in policy development, it lies in its function as a public forum for expression of the conflicting views that existed among producer organizations and between the producer and consumer organizations making up its membership. When the ABC was finally able to reach a conclusion on a policy question, it had no means of enforcing its decision. In time the producer organizations recognized its impotence, given the reluctance of the federal government to intervene in its affairs, and came to view its activities as a public relations forum not closely tied to the conduct of their operations.[24]

Such factors as independent growth and further development of blood services by regional and community blood services, changes in blood service management and management methods, scientific advances, and greater federal involvement in setting and enforcing standards brought about most of the changes in the blood system during the 1970s. The ABC's role was neither central nor crucial.

Bureau of Biologics. In 1975, influenced by several studies conducted in the early 1970s and by public pressure arising from the perceived relation between commercially obtained blood and posttransfusion hepatitis, the Bureau of Biologics proposed a new regulation requiring that whole blood and red cells bear labels distinguishing the source of the blood as either paid or volunteer and that the label for paid blood include a warning of the higher associated risk of transfusion-related hepatitis.[25] This action, aimed at segmenting the blood supply and limiting the participation of commercial services in the blood products sector, was followed by an outburst of debate among agencies and individuals who either defended the proposed regulation for its intention of reducing the rate of transfusion-related hepatitis or attacked it for its expected effects of reducing supply and restraining competition.

In 1976, after many studies and much debate, the bureau issued the regulation. Some of its effects were soon evident: over the next few years the percentage of whole blood and red cells supplied by commercial sources fell dramatically, so that by 1980 virtually all commercial services had ceased to function in the blood products sector.

Changes in the Blood System: 1971 to 1980

Many changes occurred in the national blood system during the 1970s, changes that resolved some of the issues that had prompted the National Blood Policy, partially resolved others, but left still others virtually untouched. A comparison of the performance of the blood system in 1971 and in 1980 discloses the extent to which the aims of the National Blood Policy were realized in the 1970s.

Supply. Supply underwent major changes in the 1970s (table 1). Total whole blood units collected by the blood products sector increased from 8.8 million units in 1971 to 11.15 million units in 1980, a 26.7 percent increase, more than twice the rate of the population increase for approximately the same period. This rapid growth was accompanied by much greater growth in total units transfused. Whereas in 1971 only 0.84 units of whole blood or blood components were transfused per unit of whole blood collected, by 1980 the ratio had risen to 1.32:1, an increase of 57.1 percent. The composition of transfusions also

TABLE 1

CHANGES IN SUPPLY OF WHOLE BLOOD AND BLOOD COMPONENTS IN
THE UNITED STATES, 1971 TO 1980
(thousands of units)

	1971	1980	Change (percent)
Whole blood units collected	8,800	11,150[a]	−26.7
Transfusions			
Whole blood	4,972	1,912	−61.5
Red blood cells	1,394	8,038	476.6
Platelets	410	2,842	593.2
Fresh-frozen plasma	183	1,531	736.6
Cryoprecipitated AHF	405	408	0.7
Yield: components transfused per whole blood unit collected	0.84	1.32	57.1
Whole blood collected by			
Regional and community blood centers	6,039	9,673	60.2
Hospitals	1,579	1,059	−32.9
Commercial sources	964	17	−98.2
Other	218	401[a]	83.9
Whole blood collected from			
Volunteer donors	7,836	10,917[a]	39.3
Paid donors	964	233	−75.8
Population of the United States	203,300[b]	226,500	11.4

a. Includes 270,000 units of voluntarily donated red cells imported from Europe. Total U.S. collections were 10,880,000 units.
b. 1970 census.
SOURCES: National Heart and Lung Institute, *Summary Report*; and Surgenor and Schnitzer, *Nation's Blood Resource*.

changed markedly, from dominance by whole blood units to dominance by red cell components. Regional and community blood centers led blood collection increases in the 1970s while collections from other sources (hospitals, commercial collectors, and others) declined sharply in absolute as well as in relative importance. By the end of the decade regional and community blood centers accounted for 88.9 percent of all whole blood collections in the United States, hospitals for 9.7 percent, commercial sources for less than 0.2 percent, and other sources (principally military) for 1.2 percent. Finally, the 1970s saw near elimination of the paid donor from the whole blood and blood components sector, as the percentage of whole blood units supplied by paid donors declined from 11.0 percent in 1971 to 2.1 percent in 1980.[26]

How did these changes affect the supply issues that had prompted the issuance of the National Blood Policy in 1973? The evidence on shortages is indirect and mixed. Since blood centers and blood banks do not usually measure the frequency or extent of stock shortages, only anecdotal evidence and indirect measures of stocks are available for the 1971–1980 period. Between 1971 and 1980, transfusions of whole blood and red cells, which are interchangeable, increased by 56.3 percent, platelets by 593.2 percent, and fresh-frozen plasma by 736.6 percent, while cryoprecipitated AHF transfusions remained virtually constant. Thus, except for cryoprecipitated AHF, which was being supplanted during this period by dry concentrate AHF, blood component transfusions increased up to sixty-five times as much as the population, indicating greater access and less likelihood of severe shortages.

The transfusion of red cells, platelets, fresh-frozen plasma, and cryoprecipitated AHF grew rapidly during the 1970s. The widely available supplies of components indicate a more effective use of the whole blood resource, which came about through the growth of regional and community blood centers. These centers, which increased their share of whole blood collections to almost 90 percent by 1980, were also responsible for making components readily available to hospitals in the areas they served. Moreover, by the late 1970s both the American Red Cross and the Council of Community Blood Centers had adopted the principle of community responsibility, thereby assuring patients of needed components without restrictions as to assurance coverage or payment of a nonreplacement fee.

Elimination of the paid donor was an aim of the National Blood Policy nearly realized by 1980. All ARC and CCBC centers and all AABB hospital blood banks and community blood centers, except those grandfathered by the AABB in the early 1970s to continue the use of paid donors, restricted their collections to voluntary donors. In addition, the Bureau of Biologics through labeling requirements for paid and voluntary blood and the states through labeling and liability exemption legislation made it nearly impossible for commercial centers to continue to function in the blood products sector. At the same time, growth in commercial harvesting of blood and plasma in the blood derivatives sector—which was even faster than growth in the blood products sector—coupled with restrictions on the importation of plasma provided an alternative market for commercial collectors.[27] This was a market in which nonprofit collectors were unable to compete effectively and in which the use of paid donors was not restricted.

Available evidence suggests that use of the nonreplacement fee was declining during the latter part of the 1970s. In 1979 some 30 percent of the hospitals responding to the question about the nonreplacement fee on the census by the National Heart, Lung, and Blood Institute stated that they used the fee; in 1980, however, only 21 percent of the respondents did so.[28] Moreover, by 1980 both the ARC and the CCBC had adopted the principle of community responsibility. Members of these two organizations accounted for over two-thirds of all blood units collected in 1980.[29]

Despite this record of accomplishment, several supply problems remained in 1980. The twenty-one-day shelf life for whole blood and red cells continued to create periodic shortages during the holiday and late summer periods. That period with its attendant outdating risk kept inventories from building appreciably in anticipation of such shortages. One-unit transfusions continued to be a problem. And the issues of responsibility for total community supply and community versus individual responsibility continued to exist in more subdued form.

Quality. Improvements in quality of the blood resource from 1971 to 1983 are considered at length in chapter 2. Here it is sufficient to report that methods for detection in whole blood or plasma of the hepatitis B antigen (HBsAg) by specific testing improved from 20 to 30 percent effectiveness in 1971 to over 90 percent by 1980.[30] Since hepatitis B accounted for 20 to 30 percent of all posttransfusion hepatitis, its near elimination as a source of transfusion-related disease was a major accomplishment.[31] Unfortunately, the hepatitis situation proved more complex than was realized in the early 1970s. One or more other disease-causing organisms, now referred to as hepatitis non-A, non-B (NANB), have been identified as the causes of the remaining transfusion-related hepatitis. Since the viral organisms have not been identified, no specific tests for their presence in blood are available. Only nonspecific means are used to screen donors and donated blood for the presence of NANB.

The situation with respect to regulation and enforcement of compliance with blood banking standards had improved materially by 1980. In the early 1970s approximately one of every five blood banks was subject only to state regulation and enforcement. By 1980 all blood banks were required to be registered and licensed by the Bureau of Biologics, whose standards and inspection programs had improved appreciably during the preceding decade. A similar program of regulation and enforcement was initiated by the bureau in the late 1970s for plasmapheresis centers, which it had previously not controlled.

Thus quality accomplishments of the 1970s, in both the blood products and the blood derivatives sectors, were appreciable. What were still missing were specific means of detecting NANB organisms in blood and plasma. An effective specific test for NANB was needed to eliminate hepatitis, the major remaining source of transfusion-related disease, from the nation's blood supply.

Efficiency. Attempts to improve efficiency in the blood products sector during the 1970s had mixed results. Considerable progress was made in reducing the frequency of outdated and lost units and the volume of hospital collections, which tended to lead to outdating because of the supply-demand imbalances they created among blood types; but little progress was made in settling the issue of control over blood in hospital inventories.

Outdated and lost units in 1971 and in 1980 are shown in table 2.[32] The frequency of outdated units per whole blood unit collected in 1980 was little more than half what it was in 1971, and the frequency of lost units was less than one-fourth. Overall, there was nearly a

TABLE 2

OUTDATED AND LOST WHOLE BLOOD AND RED CELL UNITS, 1971 AND 1980

	1971		1980	
	Number (thousands)	% of total collected	Number (thousands)	% of total collected
Outdated units	1,210	13.8	790	7.1
Lost units	1,230	14.0	360	3.2
Total	2,440	27.8	1,150	10.3

SOURCE: Surgenor and Schnitzer, *Nation's Blood Resource*.

two-thirds reduction in waste of whole blood units collected, a substantial accomplishment given the fact that many blood centers continued to employ collection procedures requiring adherence to a twenty-one-day shelf life.

Hospital collections of whole blood, which in 1971 accounted for 18 percent of all blood collected, fell to 9.7 percent of the total by 1980, a relative decline of 46 percent. This decline had two beneficial aspects: it helped reduce the rate of outdated and lost units, and it demonstrated the value of mobile collections. Hospitals were generally inefficient blood collectors because their small volumes tended to produce an imbalance between collections and demands by blood type during the twenty-one-day dating period. The proportionate increase during the 1970s in collections by regional and community blood centers, which served numerous hospitals and had less difficulty in matching collections and transfusions, contributed substantially to the reduction of outdating and lost units.

The growth in collections by regional and community blood centers was accomplished largely through mobile collections, in which equipment and personnel are transported to the donor group rather than having individual donors come to the hospital or collection center. Mobile collections accounted for 70 percent of all collections in 1980 and 76.4 percent of blood collected by regional and community centers.[33] They not only had higher yields per day than fixed sites but helped tap a source that had been difficult to reach—large-scale commercial, industrial, and nonprofit organizations. Moreover, access to these organizations was made more effective by use of the management abilities of their members, who planned and helped conduct the collection visits, recruited donors, and maintained records. Thus, through mobiles, the centers were able to replace the supply lost through declines in hospital and commercial collections.

During the 1970s most blood centers had only limited control over blood stored in hospital inventories. Two conditions needed to achieve control were missing: ownership of the blood by the center until transfusion and daily information on the status of inventories. Regional and community blood centers continued to transfer title to blood to the hospitals upon initial distribution. Without legal control over the blood or information about inventories, the centers had no way of managing blood resources in times of shortage.

In 1979 the Bureau of Biologics approved the use of a new blood preservative called CPDA-1, which extended the legal shelf life of whole blood and red cells from twenty-one to thirty-five days. Because of delays by the bureau in permitting use of the preservative for the collection of platelets and by bag manufacturers in producing enough bags to meet the demand, the benefits were not fully realized until 1981. Nevertheless, the preservative substantially reduced outdating and lost units in 1980, as shown in table 3.[34] From 1979 to 1980 outdating declined by 14 percent, lost units by 43 percent, and outdating and lost units combined by 26 percent. This constituted a major improvement in efficiency.

Access. Access to blood resources improved in the 1970s because of increased assurance of sufficient supplies of components and derivatives for patients in need of substantial amounts of both, especially hemophiliacs, and because of the creation of special care facilities for hemophiliacs.[35] Access was also affected by shifts in the charges for collection and replacement of blood by various organizations engaged in these activities.

In the early 1970s the long-term outlook for the treatment of hemophiliacs and for the supply of AHF was questionable.[36] A substantial portion of the AHF needed to treat hemophiliacs came in the form of cryoprecipitated AHF produced in hospitals and blood centers by a mechanical freezing and centrifuging process. This process, markedly superior to its ethanol predecessor, was supplanted in the 1970s by chemical fractionation, which produced a lyophilized (dried) form of AHF that could be easily stored and reconstituted when needed by adding sterile water. It also varied less in activity than cryoprecipitated AHF. Production of cryoprecipitated AHF was almost exactly the same in 1980 as in 1971, but the production of dry concentrate AHF had risen markedly, so that by 1980 it accounted for approximately 85 percent of the total AHF supply.[37]

In 1975 the federal government authorized the establishment of more than twenty federally funded hemophiliac care centers in the United States.[38] These centers provide the special treatment with AHF

TABLE 3

OUTDATED AND LOST UNITS, 1979 AND 1980

(thousands)

	1979	1980	Change (percent)
Total blood units collected	11,080	11,150	0.6
Outdated units	920	790	−14.1
Lost units	630	360	−42.9
Outdated plus lost units	1,550	1,150	−25.8

SOURCE: Surgenor and Schnitzer, *Nation's Blood Resource.*

products required by many hemophiliacs. They were also responsible for developing and implementing home care programs.

The decline in hospital blood collections and increase in collections by regional and community blood centers had further benefits insofar as hospital charges to patients were concerned. In his study of such charges in 1971 by hospital blood banks, community blood centers, and commercial producers, Cumming showed that hospital blood banks charged much higher average combined processing and nonreplacement fees per unit of blood transfused than did community or commercial banks.[39] The first three lines of table 4 show the results of Cumming's studies. The table includes information on average processing fees in 1972 at fifty-nine ARC regions. The average processing fee plus the nonreplacement fee, where applicable, was greatest for blood collected through hospital blood banks and least for blood collected by ARC regions. Collection by a community blood center reduced the total processing plus nonreplacement fee below the hospital average by 12 percent, and collection by a commercial producer reduced it by 33 percent. Clearly, the decline in relative importance of hospital blood bank collections helped keep down the increases in charges for blood in the 1970s.

Completely comparable data on charges are not available for 1980, but in their 1980 study of hospital charges Wallace and Wallace compared average charges for transfusion of a unit of red cells by hospitals that collected some blood with average charges by hospitals that were fully dependent on regional or community blood centers, as well as differences in charges between hospitals that did and did not use the nonreplacement fee.[40] Three findings of this study are relevant.

TABLE 4

AVERAGE TRANSFUSION CHARGES, BY TYPE OF BLOOD BANK, 1971
(fees in dollars)

Type of Blood Bank	No.	Average Volume	Average Processing Fee	Average Nonreplacement Fee	Combined Fee	Index
Hospital	690	3,000	8.80	23.72	32.52	100
Community	86	21,400	13.08	15.56	28.64	88
Commercial	5	19,800	11.27	10.67	21.94	67
ARC region	59	60,400	13.03	0	13.03	40

SOURCE: Cumming, "National Blood Policy"; and American Red Cross annual blood center operations reports.

- Hospitals that collected some of the blood they transfused had combined average processing and nonreplacement fees of $73.12 and average total fees of $92.07; noncollecting hospitals had combined average processing and nonreplacement fees of $62.11 and average total fees of $87.14.
- Hospitals that charged the nonreplacement fee had average total fees, the nonreplacement fee included, of $105.51; hospitals that did not charge the nonreplacement fee had average total fees of $84.86.
- Hospitals that charged the nonreplacement fee had average total fees, the nonreplacement fee excluded, of $77.54; hospitals that did not charge the nonreplacement fee had average total fees of $84.86.

Since the combined fee is what the patient is charged for a unit of blood, hospitals collecting at least some of their total blood supply had significantly higher average fees than those that depended entirely on regional or community blood centers.

The influence of the nonreplacement fee on the total charge to the patient can also be seen. Use of the fee as a penalty for nonreplacement and as a means of covering the costs of recruiting donors significantly raised the total charge to the patient. If the patient replaced the transfused blood, the charge by hospitals that used the nonreplacement fee was significantly less than the average charge by hospitals that did not use the fee.

Finally, growing acceptance of the community responsibility principle during the 1970s, particularly its acceptance by the ARC and the CCBC, dramatically reduced dependence on the various forms of assurance that predominated in the early 1970s. Community responsibility, which provided at cost whatever amounts of blood patients needed without regard to bank credits or membership in an assured donor group, opened access to blood resources to all members of the community. Hospitals did not need to seek out alternative sources of blood or to use the nonreplacement fee. By 1980 over two-thirds of the nation's blood supply was accessible to all on a community responsibility basis.[41]

Information. Two of the major policies set forth in the National Blood Policy were to "encourage, foster and support development of data and information collection and processing systems which will identify and describe all elements and functions in the blood banking sphere on a continuing basis" and "encouraging, fostering, and supporting activities to develop accounting and reporting systems which identify the relationship between the costs and charges for all services and materials associated with transfusion therapy."[42]

Several efforts in these respects were made during the latter half of the 1970s by task forces of the American Blood Commission. One task force endeavored to develop a uniform accounting and costing system for blood services. Another set about developing measures for evaluating the performance of regional and community blood centers. And a third established the National Blood Data Center within the ABC as a permanent, self-financing activity engaged in collecting, analyzing, and reporting financial and operating data from blood services throughout the country. Although the task forces completed the work assigned to them, they were generally unsuccessful. Blood service organizations were unwilling to implement their recommendations or to support the data center. The only real success achieved was the conduct of the 1979 and 1980 blood censuses by the National Blood Data Center, which was disbanded once they were completed.

Much the same was true of efforts during the latter half of the 1970s to develop and extend computer-based management information systems in the regions, community centers, and hospital blood banks. Several regions and community centers did eventually develop comprehensive management information systems similar to those developed under the original NHLI study, and a few hospitals tested some proprietary blood bank information systems. These efforts, however, were few, widely scattered, and, in the case of the hospitals, unsuccessful.

Recent Developments in Blood Services

Although the 1970s saw numerous advances in blood therapy and in the organization and development of blood services, events of the 1980s have followed a more mixed pattern. There have been some notable achievements, but at the same time new problems and new issues have arisen to cloud the outlook for patients and blood service organizations. What has brought about this shift in events? And what does the shift portend? Answers to the first question are readily available; answers to the second, however, are not. It is apparent that both the blood products and the blood derivatives sectors are undergoing and will continue to undergo major changes throughout the 1980s, changes that are likely to require substantial readjustments in the organization and modes of operation of blood services units.

Four forces have produced this altered outlook for the blood system:

- the AIDS crisis
- advances in alternative technologies

- maturation of the markets for blood products and some blood derivatives
- federally imposed hospital cost controls

Only the first of these forces, the AIDS crisis, is a clear threat to patients and blood services alike. Advances in technologies should be beneficial to patients but of mixed benefit and loss to the blood services. The third and fourth forces, market maturation and cost controls, threaten blood services far more than they do patients.

The AIDS Crisis and Hepatitis Non-A, Non-B. Although most people are aware of the AIDS crisis, they have little knowledge of the extent to which the nation's blood supply is at risk from it, in part because media attention has focused on the sensational aspects, favoring an anecdotal rather than an epidemiological approach to the problem, and in part because data have accumulated so slowly that reasonably reliable information is only now available. By mid-1984 certain facts about AIDS had emerged.

- It is a disease closely associated with specific urban populations: homosexuals, drug abusers, Haitian immigrants, and hemophiliacs.
- It is a viral disease, apparently caused by one or more viruses identified as HTLV III or LAV.
- It is transmitted by body fluids (saliva, semen, blood).
- Probabilities of transmission to the average blood recipient are estimated at 1:250,000 and to the average hemophiliac at 1:500.
- The incubation period is between eighteen and twenty-four months.
- No specific or reliable nonspecific tests exist for detection of the disease-causing virus or its surrogates in donors or donated blood.
- It is currently an incurable disease that ultimately causes the death of the majority of symptomatic patients.
- The secretary of health and human services has recently estimated that a specific test for the presence of HTLV III in blood will be available by 1985.

Public concern about AIDS and the likelihood of its contaminating the nation's blood supply arises both from estimates of its mortality rate—90 percent in four years—and from the diseases, such as cancer and pneumonia, that accompany it.

Table 5 contains information on all cases of AIDS reported to the Centers for Disease Control (CDC) by August 1984.[43] There have been seventy-nine cases among blood recipients. During the reporting period approximately 59 million units of whole blood or red cells were transfused to about 19 million patients. The incidence rate of the

111

TABLE 5

REPORTED CASES OF AIDS, BY PATIENT GROUP, 1979–AUGUST 1984

Patient Group	Adults/Adolescents	Children	Total	Percent
Homosexuals	4,060	0	4,060	71.2
Drug abusers	984	0	984	17.3
Haitians	223	0	223	3.9
Recipients of blood transfusions	66	13	79	1.4
Hemophiliacs	38	4	42	0.7
Other	265	46	311	5.5
Total	5,636	63	5,699	100.0

SOURCE: Centers for Disease Control.

disease, therefore, has been about four cases per million blood recipients—that is, about a 1:250,000 chance of contracting the disease from a blood transfusion. Hemophiliacs, most of whom are treated with lyophilized AHF, are at much greater risk. Some 20,000 hemophiliacs are now under treatment in the United States; so the forty-two reported cases of AIDS among these patients amount to an incidence rate of about 1:500. Since lyophilized AHF is a blood derivative, hemophiliacs should not be included among whole blood or red cell recipients in assessing the risks of this disease for blood recipients.

AIDS is less of a threat to the nation's blood recipients than hepatitis B and hepatitis non-A, non-B (NANB), which have received little media attention in recent years. Table 6 contains a comparison of the likelihood of a blood recipient's contracting hepatitis from a blood transfusion with the likelihood of contracting AIDS and the related likelihood of an acute case or mortality. The likelihood of dying as a result of contracting hepatitis through blood transfusion is about four times as great as the likelihood of dying from AIDS, and the likelihood of contracting hepatitis is far greater than the likelihood of contracting AIDS. Clearly hepatitis, especially NANB, constitutes a greater threat to blood recipients despite present public concern over AIDS. Moreover, if identification of the AIDS-causing agent, HTLV III, is correct and development of a specific test for its presence in blood is imminent, then NANB is obviously a greater long-term threat to the blood.

Insofar as blood derivatives are concerned, the situation is quite different. Because of their production processes, albumin and immune globulins are unaffected by either disease. AHF, however, is

TABLE 6
LIKELIHOOD OF CONTRACTION OF HEPATITIS AND AIDS FOR BLOOD
RECIPIENTS AND RELATED LIKELIHOOD OF MORBIDITY AND
MORTALITY, 1984

	Hepatitis B/ NANB	AIDS
Likelihood of contracting the disease	1:10[a]	1:250,000
Likelihood of contracting an acute case of the disease	1:2,000[b]	1:250,000
Likelihood of mortality as a result of the disease	1:75,000[c]	1:275,000[d]

a. Based on ALT elevation test results from recent studies.
b. Based on ARC reported rate of 5.5/10,000 patients.
c. Based on CDC reported rate of 2.5 percent for blood recipients.
d. Based on 90 percent mortality rate, as reported by CDC.
SOURCE: American Red Cross and Centers for Disease Control.

affected, and the risks of AIDS infection as a result of AHF infusion are increased appreciably by the practice of pooling source plasma in the manufacture of AHF. In addition, the frequency of infusion of AHF in hemophiliacs, especially as a means of avoiding soft tissue hemorrhage, increases the risk of contracting AIDS. For these reasons hemophiliacs and their spokesmen have been leaders in efforts to restrain collection of blood and plasma from high-risk populations and advocates of nonspecific tests and other screening procedures using confidential questionnaires and call-up procedures to eliminate donations from high-risk populations. More recently blood derivatives firms have been heat-treating AHF to reduce the risks of disease at the cost of some reduction in activity and an increase in price. Some physicians attending hemophiliacs have shifted treatment to management of hemorrhages and others have resorted to greater use of cryoprecipitate.

Although no specific tests are available to detect the presence in donors or donated blood or plasma of AIDS or NANB, nonspecific tests for the surrogates of each have been proposed. For AIDS three such nonspecific tests have been advanced, two of which have been introduced in some hospitals and blood centers in high-risk areas. Given the uncertainties about the effectiveness of these tests in detecting AIDS and the high rates of false positives they produce, their use appears to have been motivated as much by the threat of personal and institutional liability if blood recipients contract AIDS as by belief in the ability of the tests to reduce risks of the disease. For NANB present evidence suggests that alinine aminotransferase (ALT) testing, now used by some blood centers, can reduce the risks of transfusion-related NANB. Members of the Greater New York Blood Program, which uses the ALT test, have estimated that the test reduces the probabilities of NANB infection by a third at a cost of a 2 percent loss of blood collected.[44] Most regional and community blood centers, however, have not adopted ALT testing because of its costs and incomplete data on its effectiveness. No randomized prospective study has shown that exclusion of blood from donors with elevated ALT levels lowers the incidence of posttransfusion hepatitis.[45] There appears little prospect of short-term resolution of the NANB detection problem because the disease-causing agent or agents have yet to be identified.

In summary, while AIDS is not yet a major threat to the nation's blood supply, it has been an exceedingly disruptive force in the system, curtailing collections in certain higher-risk areas, raising prospects of demands on hospitals and blood services for directed and autologous donations, and creating substantial apprehension among recipients of blood products and blood system managers. For hemophiliacs, the AIDS threat is much greater than for blood recipients and has led to curtailment of treatment and to production of a somewhat less effective heat-treated AHF and the use of other, less risky modes of therapy. For NANB, which continues to be a serious threat to blood recipients, ALT testing may offer some benefits, although its effectiveness and the cost-benefit trade-off from its use remain in question.

Advances in Technology. Recent advances in blood technology have been of substantial benefit to blood services organizations. Other advances now in prospect threaten some present forms of operation. All the advances, however, have been or promise to be of benefit to blood recipients.

Advances that have had or are expected to have significant effects on blood service operations are

- the introduction of CPDA-1 as a preservative for blood products
- the development of recombinant DNA techniques for the production of blood derivatives and monoclonal antibody techniques for the production of immunization products
- the development of chemical substitutes for red cells

CPDA-1 has been beneficial to both blood service organizations and blood recipients; recombinant DNA and monoclonal techniques are of prospective benefit to blood recipients but a threat to present producers of blood products and blood derivatives; and prospects of a chemical substitute for red cells are of uncertain benefit to blood recipients and a potential source of major loss to existing blood services.

The introduction of CPDA-1 as a preservative for blood products was completed in 1981. Partial implementation of this technology in 1980 significantly reduced outdating and lost units. The rate of reduction from 1979 to 1981 has been estimated at almost 50 percent.[46] Moreover, because of the added fourteen days of shelf life for whole blood and red cells, average inventories rose approximately 34 percent, reducing the average frequency of normal shortages by 59 percent and of emergency shortages by 64 percent.[47] Thus CPDA-1 substantially increased the supply of whole blood and red cells, improved the efficiency of blood service operations, virtually eliminated holiday shortages, substantially reduced summer shortages, and helped to produce an excess of collections over transfusions in some regions. Those regions have become net exporters of whole blood and red cells to regions that continue to experience chronic shortages. In brief, CPDA-1 has been a benefit to all achieved at relatively low cost above the costs of the research leading to its development.

Recent development of recombinant DNA techniques for the production of albumin and AHF and of monoclonal techniques for producing specific antibodies that will function more effectively than immune globulins poses a threat to present producers of blood derivatives and blood products.[48] These techniques have not yet reached the stage of commercial implementation, but one or both will probably do so within the next few years. When they do, and if they prove economically feasible, the direct threat is to present producers of albumin, AHF, and immune globulins. Since most of the organizations developing the new techniques are not now producers of blood derivatives, successful development may bring into the markets new competitors having comparative advantages over the present producers. The advantages may be economic, in that the new techniques will be of lower cost than those now in use, or qualitative, in that the derivatives will not carry with them the risks of disease, or both.

Successful implementation of these techniques will also have an indirect but substantial effect on present producers of blood products, because much of the source plasma now used to produce AHF and immune globulins and of the recovered plasma used to produce albumin comes from the blood products sector. Success of the new technologies would dramatically reduce the demand for both source and recovered plasma and thereby reduce the revenues received by blood centers and other blood products organizations for them. This

115

reduction in revenue would be disproportionately larger than any reduction in costs of plasma collection and recovery, so that the excess of present revenues from plasma sales over the added costs of collecting and separating the plasma would have to be borne by other blood products or services, such as whole blood, red cells, platelets, and consultation. Moreover, the availability of specific antibodies produced by monoclonal techniques should reduce the demand for fresh-frozen plasma and thus reduce the marginal income available to cover the costs of other blood products. The prices of blood products not in competition with those produced by recombinant DNA and monoclonal techniques would then increase, an undesirable effect for the recipients of those other blood products and the organizations that produce them.

Prospects for a chemical substitute for red cells for the purpose of oxygen transport are poor despite publicity recently given to the development of perfluorochemicals for this purpose.[49] Such chemicals have a number of adverse indications, including respiratory and toxicity complications. Because present perfluorides must be frozen while stored and are effective only in an oxygen-rich environment, they must be administered under strict hospital conditions. They are also excreted rapidly, so that benefits are short term unless they are re-administered continuously. Given these conditions, prospects for successful development of a red cell substitute for general use are low. In the near future the present substitute or its successors will be used primarily in those few instances where the patient is in urgent need of enhanced oxygen transport and refuses for religious or other reasons to accept a red cell transfusion.

Maturation of the Markets for Blood Products and Blood Derivatives. During the 1970s a principal aim of the blood system was to increase the supply of blood products and services to fulfill large and ever-rising demands. In the 1980s, however, existing supplies of whole blood, red cells, and albumin seem more than adequate to meet demand, and demand is likely to rise relatively slowly. It is a classic case of growth in supply capacity suddenly meeting and exceeding demand with the result that the historical rate of growth in supply is no longer a reasonable guide to future expectations. Excess regional supplies of whole blood and red cells have begun to appear frequently in recent years, and more regions and community blood centers have entered the resupply markets, shipping blood products from one region or community center to another to dispose of their excess production.[50]

A further complication for blood services organizations is the recent decline in the rate of increase of total product yields from a unit of whole blood. During the 1970s increases in the product yield ratio (that is, the average number of units of product produced per unit of whole blood collected) were of major benefit to blood services organizations, since these products were produced at added costs well below the revenues received from their sale. Present demands for component products, though still growing, are doing so only slightly, yield ratios are nowhere near their theoretical maximums, and it appears that most of the attainable growth in yield has already been realized.[51] As a consequence this previously important source of income to blood centers is likely to be seriously curtailed, adding significantly to pressures on centers to find other sources of revenue or to improve operating efficiency to meet rising costs.

Obviously, maturation of these markets is likely to be advantageous for whole blood, red cell, and albumin recipients because it assures them of any needed supply and of stronger competition among the producers, raising the possibility that charges may fall or at least not rise as fast as they would otherwise have risen. Since whole blood and red cells are the main revenue- and income-producing products of all regional and community blood centers, excess supply capacities for both are likely to lead to efforts by surplus suppliers to dump their surpluses in other regions or communities at prices below those charged by present suppliers in those regions. Surpluses are also likely to lead some hospitals to seek new sources of supply outside their regions or communities either directly or through buying cooperatives, thereby inducing added competition. Thus a considerable increase in competition in the production and distribution of whole blood and red cells is likely.

Since increased competition in and between regions in whole blood and red cells is likely to lead to lower prices, or at least a lower rate of increase in prices, blood centers will need to shift the burden of common production and distribution costs to other products and services, such as platelets, fresh plasma, leukocytes, cryoprecipitate, and consultation. If this is not wholly possible, blood services will also need to improve their productive and distributive efficiency to compensate for the effects of increased competition. Another result is likely to be the unbundling of services, so that blood centers are forced to charge for the laboratory and consultation services they now provide without separate charge. Since only certain hospitals require these services, those that do not need them are likely to press for the elimination of this portion of the charges.

On balance these competitive changes should be of benefit to blood recipients, although recipients in need of blood products not in excess supply, or of services now provided at no additional charge, may find their charges increased while those in need of competitive products, or not in need of special services, may find their charges reduced. Overall, however, the principal social benefit will come through improvements in efficiency induced by increased competition.

Federally Imposed Hospital Cost Controls. A recent change in the health care industry that is not the result of technical advances but is likely to have similar effects is the imposition of federal hospital cost controls. These controls, based on diagnosis-related groups (DRGs), provide hospitals with fixed amounts of compensation from Medicare and Medicaid to cover the costs of treating patients for each of 467 categories of diseases or other conditions requiring hospital treatment. With the introduction of DRGs, hospitals now have direct incentives to reduce the costs of treating each Medicare or Medicaid patient, either by reducing the use of products or services or by reducing the length of hospital stay. Since blood products, blood derivatives, and other blood services are all sources of hospital costs, hospitals have an incentive to seek ways of reducing those costs. Some obvious ways of doing so are to reduce the quantities of blood products and derivatives used to treat patients to the amounts minimally necessary, to seek alternative sources at lower costs, and to bring pressure on regional and community blood centers through community advisory committees to keep their prices in reasonable accord with those of other regions and centers with lower prices.

In brief, the imposition of DRGs, together with alternative methods of producing blood derivatives, maturation of market demands for whole blood and red cells, and the decline in the rate of increase of yield ratios, is likely to cause a substantial increase in economic competition in these markets, which will ultimately lead to a search for new products and services and to a reorganization of the structure and functioning of many blood products organizations. All in all, the outlook is for a different state of affairs in the national blood system from that of the 1970s. Instead of steady growth and continuous development of regional and community blood centers, the expectation is for less growth coupled with increased financial pressure on the weaker blood services, perhaps eventually leading to consolidations by either merger or takeover.

Notes

1. Richard Titmuss, *The Gift Relationship* (London: Allen and Unwin, 1971).
2. See references cited ibid., pp. 47–69, 142–57.

3. Paul Cumming, "National Blood Policy and the American Blood Commission" (Ph.D. dissertation, State University of New York at Buffalo, 1976).

4. Ibid., p. 266. American Red Cross, *Blood Center Operations, 1965 to 1971* Washington, D.C.

5. See Donald Walz, "An Effective Hospital Transfusion Committee," *Journal of the American Medical Association*, August 31, 1964; and idem, "Changing Blood Transfusion Trends in the United States," *Journal, News of Blood Programme in Canada*, April 1984.

6. Ian Mitchell, *Basis for the National Blood Policy*, document distributed March 24, 1977, in response to criticisms of the need for the National Blood Policy; cites as key sources of conditions in 1960s and early 1970s: William Miller and Paul Schmidt, "National Blood Program as of 1969," *Pathologist*, vol. 23, no. 9, pp. 289–94; Ad Hoc Committee on Component Therapy, Committee on Plasma and Plasma Substitutes, *An Evaluation of the Utilization of Human Blood Resources in the United States*, National Academy of Sciences, National Research Council, October 1970.

7. See, for example, *New York Times*, March 26, 1962; "Blood Procurement in the Chicago Area—an Update," *Laboratory Medicine*, May 1977; and Kenneth Fraundorf, "Competition in Blood Banking," *Public Policy*, Spring 1975.

8. National Heart and Lung Institute, *Summary Report: NHLI's Blood Resources Studies*, Department of Health, Education, and Welfare, 1972.

9. See, for example, Edward Wallace and Carl Pegels, *Summary Report: Analysis and Design of a Model Regional Blood Management System*, report to NHLI, February 28, 1972.

10. Titmuss, *The Gift Relationship*, pp. 142–54.

11. National Heart and Lung Institute, *Summary Report*.

12. Ibid.; and John Jennings, *An Introduction to Blood Banking Systems*, Technical Report no. 21, Operations Research Institute, Massachusetts Institute of Technology, July 1966.

13. Wallace and Pegels, *Summary Report*.

14. See, for example, Massachusetts Department of Public Health, "Blood Use in Massachusetts," *New England Journal of Medicine*, February 25, 1971, p.447.

15. See, for example, National Health Council, "The Changing Role of the Public and Private Sectors in Health," *Report of the 1973 National Health Forum*, March 1973; William Kuhns, "Improving the Use of Hospital Blood Services," *Hospital Practice*, April 1970; and Gregory Palermo, Joseph Bove, and Alfred Katz, "Patterns of Blood Use in Connecticut," *Transfusion*, November–December 1980.

16. National Heart and Lung Institute, *Summary Report*.

17. Department of Health, Education, and Welfare, "National Blood Policy," *Federal Register*, vol. 39, no. 47, March 8, 1974; and Ian Mitchell, *Background Information on National Blood Policy*, document distributed by Department of Health, Education, and Welfare, July 20, 1973.

18. The community responsibility principle was adopted in 1972 by both the American Red Cross and the Council of Community Blood Centers.

19. National Heart and Lung Institute, *Studies of Applications of Electronic Data Processing to Blood Management*, July 1972.

20. Reuben Kessel, "Transfused Blood, Serum Hepatitis, and the Coase Theorem," *Journal of Law and Economics*, vol. 17, no. 2 (October 1974).

21. Department of Health, Education, and Welfare, "National Blood Policy," *Federal Register*, vol. 39, no. 176, September 10, 1976.

22. Ibid.

23. See ibid., detailed plans for formation of the American Blood Commission.

24. Joel Solomon, "Expecting the Future to Be Different from the Past," *Lab World*, January 1982; Luanne Kennedy, "National Blood Policy Survivor May Need Transfu-

sion," *Lab World*, October 1978; and General Accounting Office, *Problems in Carrying Out the National Blood Policy*, March 1978.

25. Department of Health, Education, and Welfare, *Federal Register*, vol. 42, (1977), pp. 11018–23.

26. Douglas Surgenor and Sarah Schnitzer, *The Nation's Blood Resource 1979 and 1980* (Report submitted to Division of Blood Diseases and Resources, National Heart, Lung, and Blood Institute, 1983; forthcoming).

27. Production of albumin and AHF, Factor VIII, from blood derivatives grew at rates of about 25 percent and 49 percent per annum between 1971 and 1980 according to Michael Rodell, vice-president, Revlon Health Care Group, private communication.

28. Edward Wallace and Mary Ann Wallace, *Hospital Transfusion Charges and Community Blood Center Costs* (Reports submitted to Division of Blood Diseases and Resources, National Heart, Lung, and Blood Institute, 1982; forthcoming).

29. Surgeoner and Schnitzer, *Nation's Blood Resource*.

30. Ronald Koretz and Gary Gitnick, "Prevention of Post-transfusion Hepatitis," *American Journal of Medicine*, December 1975.

31. Lewellys Barker, Roger Dodd, and Gerald Sandler, "Epidemiology of Hepatitis B and Post-transfusion and Nosocomial Hepatitis," in *Viral Hepatitis, Laboratory and Clinical Science* (New York: Marcel Decker, 1983), chap. 8; and International Forum, "How Frequent Is Post-transfusion Hepatitis after Introduction of Third Generation Donor Screening for Hepatitis B? What Is Its Probable Nature? *Vox Sanguis (1977), pp. 346–63*.

32. Surgenor and Schnitzer, *Nation's Blood Resource*.

33. Ibid.

34. Ibid.

35. Public Law 94-63, passed by Congress in 1975, authorized the establishment of comprehensive hemophilia diagnostic and treatment centers.

36. National Heart and Lung Institute, *Summary Report*.

37. Louis Aledort and Scott Goodnight, "Hemophilia Treatment: Its Relationship to Blood Products," *Progress in Hematology* (New York: Grune and Straton, 1981), vol. 12.

38. Public Law 94-63.

39. Cumming, "National Blood Policy."

40. Wallace and Wallace, *Hospital Transfusion Charges*.

41. The sum of all ARC and CCBC collections.

42. *Federal Register*, vol. 39, no. 47 (1974), p. 9329.

43. Center for Disease Control, *Weekly Surveillance Report–United States, AIDS Activity*, August 20, 1984.

44. Alan Waldman and Johanna Pindyck, "Blood Donor Alanine Aminotransferase Levels: An Automated Screening System," *Laboratory Management*, June 1983.

45. Joseph Bove, Harold Oberman, Paul Holland, Kamal Ishak, Carl Peck, and James Shorey, "Report of the Ad Hoc Committee on ALT Testing," *Transfusion*, vol. 22 (1982), pp. 4–5.

46. Paul Cumming, Edward Wallace, Robert Cerveny, and Carl Pegels, *Impact of Adenine on Blood Banking* (Report submitted to Division of Blood Diseases and Resources, NHLBI, 1983; scheduled for publication in 1984).

47. Ibid.

48. International Forum, "What Is the Prospective Impact of the Recombinant DNA Technique on the Production of Human Plasma Derivatives? Which Are the Derivatives Where Donor Plasma Could Be Replaced?" *Vox Sanguis*, vol. 44 (1983), pp. 390–95.

49. Kenneth Waxman, Kevin Tremper, Bruce Cullen, and Robert Mason, "Per-

fluorocarbon Infusion in Bleeding Patients Refusing Blood Transfusions," *Archives of Surgery*, June 1984; "FDA Committee Questions Fluosol Efficacy; U.S. Approval Not Imminent," *Medical News*, November 18, 1983.

50. Based on information on distribution of whole blood and red cells contained in American Red Cross operating reports for 1983–1984; *AABB Blood Bank Week*, August 3, 1984; report on CCBC collections in first five months of 1984; personal experience with four exporting or importing blood centers in 1981, reported in Cumming, et al., *Impact of Adenine on Blood Banking*; observations of trends in whole blood and red cell inventories of the American Red Cross, which increased from 59,322 units in 1980 to 114,602 units in 1983; and conversations with leading blood bankers in 1984.

51. Based on data developed from American Red Cross sources and included in "Improving Efficiency in a Changing Environment" (Paper presented at the Blood Services Management Conference, American Red Cross, September 13–15, 1983).

3
Blood Quality: Past and Present

In his examination of the issues, past and present, concerning blood quality Ross Eckert makes three major assertions.

- In the 1970s the nonprofit blood services used the specious argument of high risk of transfusion-related hepatitis from paid blood to eliminate their competitors, the commercial blood services, from the blood products market.
- Present methods used by the American Red Cross to recruit donors bring about unnecessarily high risks of transfusion-related disease.
- Encouraging paid donors and commercial blood services to reenter the blood products market would lessen overall risks of transfusion-related disease.

Each of these assertions rests on the premise that the risks of transfusion-related disease from paid donors were and still are incompletely analyzed and understood and as a consequence overstated in comparison with the risks from volunteer blood.

Further investigation of conditions in the 1970s and now, however, shows that both were and are different from those described by Eckert and more complicated.

Paid Donor Risks and the Volunteer Blood Services in the 1970s

Were the risks of paid blood incompletely analyzed and significantly overstated in the 1970s? Did the nonprofit blood services use the argument of high risk of paid blood to gain a competitive advantage in the blood products market? Answers to these questions depend on answers to four related questions.

- Was blood obtained from paid donors in the 1970s significantly higher in transfusion-related hepatitis risk than blood obtained from volunteer donors?
- Were the aims of the Department of Health, Education, and Welfare to establish an all-volunteer donor system and the aim of the Bureau of Biologics to reduce hepatitis risk by requiring the labeling of blood reasonable given conditions at the time?

- Did arguments favoring altruism in blood donation have a significant effect on development of the National Blood Policy and the subsequent actions of the American Blood Commission and the Bureau of Biologics?
- Were the nonprofit blood services motivated primarily by a desire to achieve competitive advantage in their efforts to eliminate paid donors from the blood products market?

Transfusion-related Risks in the 1970s. Reexamination of the literature and other evidence on transfusion-related risks of hepatitis in the 1970s discloses two sets of separate but related materials: (1) studies of the 1960s and early 1970s, which influenced the formulation of the National Blood Policy, and (2) studies of the mid-1970s, which related to the labeling proposal of the Bureau of Biologics of the Food and Drug Administration.

The studies that influenced the formulation of the National Blood Policy, including its expressed aim of developing an all-volunteer donor system, were made in the 1960s and were for the most part of narrow scope. They attempted either to relate the incidence of posttransfusion hepatitis to the type of blood service employed, commercial or volunteer, or to measure the incidence of hepatitis among certain classes of persons (for example, drug addicts) known to be paid commercial donors. Among the first category were studies by Allen, by Boeve, Winterscheid, and Merendion, and by Cohen and Dougherty, all of which showed a relatively high frequency of posttransfusion hepatitis among patients transfused with blood from commercial sources.[1] In the second category were studies such as that of Allen, who in a 1966 article cited other studies showing a high incidence of serum hepatitis among drug users known to supply the commercial services.[2] These and similar studies alerted the blood services community to the risks of hepatitis from commercially obtained blood; more definitive evidence was provided by Walsh, Purcell, and Morrow in the early 1970s.[3] In a study of open-heart surgery patients at the NIH clinical center, they found that 50 percent of the patients receiving multiple transfusions of primarily commercial blood contracted hepatitis. This work was followed in 1972 by a study by the National Heart and Lung Institute (NHLI) of 4,984 cardiovascular surgery patients at fourteen university centers, in which it was found that 5.3 percent of patients receiving primarily commercial blood and only 1.4 to 1.7 percent of those receiving volunteer blood developed posttransfusion hepatitis.[4]

These studies showing a substantially higher risk of hepatitis from commercial blood had a significant effect on the formulation of the National Blood Policy. In response to private sector comments on the proposed development of an all-volunteer donor system, the HEW task force responsible for developing the policy estimated that the 10 to 15 percent of transfused blood from commerical sources was responsible for 25 to 40 percent of all overt posttransfusion hepatitis and that transfusions were responsible each year for 17,000 cases of overt hepatitis, 83,000 cases of covert hepatitis, and 850 deaths.[5] The task force associated the three to four times greater risk of commercial blood with cash payments to donors, which motivated high-risk donors to sell their blood. Given the results of its studies and other investigation, the task force felt justified in recommending an all-volunteer donor system for blood products.

These early analyses were not clear about a critical distinction between (1) the risk associated with paid donors and (2) the risk associated with commercial services. All donors to the commercial services were paid, but not all paid donors donated to commercial services. A substantial number in the 1960s and early 1970s donated to non-profit hospital blood banks and community blood services, among which it was common to use paid donors to meet emergency needs and to balance supply among the various blood types. Some nonprofit blood services depended heavily on paid donors. Most of these were respected services, such as the Milwaukee Blood Center, United Blood Services, and the Mayo clinics. They supplied substantial amounts of blood to hospitals and patients, with no evidence of hepatitis risks exceeding those experienced with volunteer donors. Some, such as Milwaukee and United Blood Services, shifted to an all-volunteer system because of events of the early and mid-1970s while others, such as Mayo, continued to use paid donors even after the issuance of the National Blood Policy.

In the 1960s and early 1970s hospitals, in particular, were common users of paid donors, frequently members of their staffs. Many volunteer blood services were not committed to the principles of full supply and community responsibility. Knowing this and doubting their ability to get all the blood they needed from the regional or community service, many hospitals maintained panels of paid donors. The practice continued in common use until the latter part of the 1970s, when issuance of the new labeling requirements by the Bureau of Biologics led most hospitals to eliminate the use of paid donors.

Most of these early studies examined the relation of hepatitis to blood obtained from commercial sources. Only the NHLI study published in 1972 differentiated between blood obtained from paid hospital donors and that obtained from paid commercial donors. This study, as shown in part in table 3 of Eckert's work, found that the incidence rate of hepatitis for blood obtained from the two paid sources was markedly different. Paid hospital blood had an average incidence approximately twice that of volunteer blood, paid commercial blood an incidence three times that of volunteer blood. Obviously, blood obtained from commercial sources was the greater problem. As both the General Accounting Office and Eckert have pointed out, the details of the 1972 NHLI study, shown in table 4 of Eckert's work, show that one commercial source had an incidence rate only slightly higher than the average of all-volunteer services and below the rates of two of the individual volunteer services. Unfortunately, a similar breakdown of incidence rates among paid hospital sources was not available. In all likelihood such an analysis would have shown a similar dispersion of rates for paid hospital donors, with the rates of some paid donor groups below that for all-volunteer groups and below the rates of some of the individual volunteer groups. The point is that blood came from three sources—all-volunteer, hospital paid, and commercial paid—and the risks of hepatitis for recipients of blood from the three categories were significantly different, that of paid commercial blood being by far the highest.

The proposal by the Bureau of Biologics in late 1975 to require that blood be labeled as paid or volunteer and that the label for paid blood state the added risk associated with its use resulted in several additional studies linking posttransfusion hepatitis to paid and volunteer blood as well as a review of some of the earlier studies. Three major new studies were produced at this time: by the National Bureau of Standards, the Department of Health, Education, and Welfare (HEW) and the General Accounting Office (GAO).[6]

The National Bureau of Standards study was concerned principally with the effect on costs of blood to the hospitals of alternative ways of organizing blood services, given different levels of hepatitis testing effectiveness. The study assumed the risk of transfusion-related hepatitis from commercial blood to be five times that of volunteer blood and the best available hepatitis testing procedure to be only 25 to 30 percent effective. It found that the typical paid donor received $8.00 per unit while under a regional system of volunteer donor recruitment, such as that developed in Milwaukee by the mid-1970s, donors could be recruited for as little as $2.90 per unit. Under a similar nationwide system the number of volunteer donors required to make up for the lost commercial supply could be obtained at an estimated cost of $4.40 per unit. The authors cautioned that elimination of paid donors, though preferable, should not be attempted before effective regional systems existed to ensure the replacement of the required supply, for "being short a unit is worse than using a paid unit."

125

The study by HEW estimated the savings from conversion to an all-volunteer blood system. This study, using several limiting assumptions about alternatives and their costs, assumed that the risk of hepatitis from paid blood was three to five times that from volunteer blood, an assumption that does not appear to have been seriously challenged by others despite their disagreement with some aspects of the study.

The study by the GAO was the most extensive of all. The GAO first reviewed the results of prior studies, including the 1972 NHLI study of 4,984 patients at fourteen university centers. It also made its own study of thirty-nine blood donor groups, twenty-one of which were volunteer and eighteen paid, in Los Angeles, Chicago, Baltimore, and the NIH clinical center and found the average risk of transfusion-related hepatitis from paid blood to be approximately three times as great as the risk from volunteer blood. Results of this study are given in tables 5 and 6 of Eckert's work. As Eckert points out, the GAO noted that a number of paid donor groups had risks of transfusion-related hepatitis significantly lower than the average for all donor groups. Pursuing this distinction further, the GAO found the same results reported by Eckert in his table 7: that paid donor groups associated with hospitals had an average rate of hepatitis about 60 percent higher than the average for all-volunteer groups while commercial and nonprofit blood banks that paid their donors had an average rate over three times that for all-volunteer groups.

The GAO went on to state that socioeconomic status in the areas from which the donors in twenty-one of its study groups came accounted for 63 percent of the explained difference in incidence of hepatitis in its study and whether donors were volunteer or paid accounted for only 36 percent of the difference. The GAO recommended (1) developing procedures to improve the quality of blood but retaining paid blood from blood banks with a valid record of supplying high-quality blood, (2) establishing a national registry for unacceptable donors, (3) testing all blood for hepatitis by the best available methods and developing new and improved methods, and (4) determining the effects of the use of frozen and fresh-washed red cells on posttransfusion hepatitis, an alternative also supported by the National Bureau of Standards study.

Actions of HEW and the Bureau of Biologics. The distinction between transfusion-related rates of hepatitis from paid hospital donors and from paid commercial donors, which the GAO endeavored to make, and the fact that paid donor groups in nonprofit hospitals such as

Mayo or the NIH clinical center had hepatitis rates below those of most volunteer services appear to have been passed over in the responses of HEW and the Bureau of Biologics to these studies and their subsequent recommendations and actions. In response to the GAO recommendations, HEW stated: "The evidence now available overwhelmingly demonstrates that more can be done to prevent transfusion-related hepatitis by total reliance on unpaid donors than by any other measure or combination of measures."[7]

Clearly HEW, the American Blood Commission, which supported its position, and the bureau, which subsequently implemented the labeling regulation, were aware that some paid donor groups had hepatitis risks not significantly higher, and in some instances actually lower, than those of many volunteer groups. Why, then, did HEW press for the labeling of all blood and the bureau proceed to require such labeling, including the paid blood warning, knowing that these actions would virtually eliminate paid donors as well as the commercial blood services? Eckert suggests that they did so because of pressure by the nonprofit volunteer services who opposed paid donors, realizing that the nonprofit services could obtain the 15 percent market share held by the commerical services. There are, however, other more plausible reasons for the actions of HEW and the bureau, reasons more compelling than the one suggested by Eckert.

The principal objective of HEW and the bureau was to achieve a substantial reduction in the relatively high rate of posttransfusion hepatitis that they clearly associated with the commercial services. These services had been shown to be the high-risk source of the disease, a fact on which all parties to the discourse agreed. That some paid donor groups, primarily those of nonprofit hospitals, had posttransfusion hepatitis rates the same as or lower than those of volunteer groups was not the important consideration. Given the absence of effective testing procedures and the known higher risks of commercial blood, health policy considerations dictated that the most direct and effective course would be to eliminate the commercial services. Direct elimination through prohibition of commercially obtained blood, however, was not possible under existing laws and regulations. What was possible was to require the labeling of all blood, knowing that such labeling would make risk-averse hospitals and physicians hesitate to use paid blood under all but exceptional circumstances. Labeling would eliminate nearly all paid blood from the market, including blood collected by those nonprofit organizations able to show that the risk of hepatitis from such blood was no greater than that of volunteer blood. The loss of this supply would be part of the costs of ridding the market of commercial blood, an event the benefits from which obviously justified the costs in the minds of those in HEW and the bureau who supported the labeling action.

About this time a study by Reuben Kessel entered the discussion.[8] Kessel, while accepting estimates of the added average risk of hepatitis associated with commercial blood, argued for its retention, proposing that all hospitals and blood services be held strictly liable for the quality of blood they transfused. He argued that strict liability would give hospitals and doctors a powerful incentive to seek high-quality sources, paid or volunteer. He estimated the value of hepatitis-free blood at $202 per unit—$150 per unit above what blood then cost— a margin that would cover any added costs of enhanced testing and registration and of insuring against awards of damages in cases where hepatitis occurred. This proposal would certainly have strongly motivated hospitals and physicians to seek blood of minimum risk. It was never seriously considered, however, for several reasons: the large amounts of litigation it would obviously create, the likelihood that its intent would be circumvented by requiring waivers from all blood recipients, and a lack of effective specific testing methods and indirect selection procedures to ensure the identification and elimination of infected donors even at markedly higher costs. Still, the proposal stimulated debate about whether the elimination of commercialism from the blood products sector was justified, particularly on altruistic grounds.

In its effort to rid the market of commercial blood, HEW was obviously less concerned with loss of the paid supply than other agencies, such as the National Bureau of Standards, the General Accounting Office, and the Council on Wage and Price Stability.[9] Through the American Blood Commission HEW had already launched programs to strengthen recruitment of volunteer donors, develop regional blood services, and support the principles of full supply and community responsibility, all of which it expected to aid in the development of the volunteer services and to enhance their ability to replace the supply lost through eliminating paid donors. At this time many of the commercial services operated mainly as supplementary suppliers to the volunteer services, providing the hospitals with limited amounts of blood and other products and services. The hospitals that used them did so because they were an alternative and at times a low-cost partial supplier. The hospitals depended on the volunteer services for the bulk of their product and service needs and apparently intended to continue this practice unless forced to do otherwise. In many instances it was less a question whether the volunteer services could replace the commercial supply than whether the hospitals would permit them to do so. Both HEW and the bureau appear to have been
128

confident that the volunteer services could replace the lost paid supply.

Opponents of the labeling regulation did not see it this way. The National Bureau of Standards and the General Accounting Office were concerned about the ability of the blood system to replace the lost commercial supply, expressing the belief that higher-risk blood was better than no blood. The GAO and the Council on Wage and Price Stability were also concerned with the loss of that portion of the paid blood supply that was of average risk or lower risk than all-volunteer blood—a cost HEW believed the blood system could bear. The council was also concerned with the effects of the lost supply on the price of blood, arguing that, *ceteris paribus*, any reduction in supply must lead to an increase in implicit price. That argument appears to have been considered arcane by others since it was based entirely on theoretical constructs unsupported by practical studies.

In its study HEW endeavored to show that the costs of overt posttransfusion hepatitis would be less under an all-volunteer system. As members of the council pointed out, this study was flawed by the assumption that the lost paid blood could be replaced by the volunteer services at zero net additional cost. In fact, no one had a reasonable basis for estimating what the incremental cost of replacing the supply was likely to be. HEW appears to have been confident, however, that the labeling action would not lead to a shortage, that the volunteer services could fill the gap, and that the added costs, whatever they might be, would be justified by the reduced rate of posttransfusion hepatitis.

The position taken by the Council on Wage and Price Stability in this discourse was almost identical with that now taken by Eckert. The council did not question that the average incidence of posttransfusion hepatitis from commercial blood was substantially higher than the incidence from other blood and that all blood recipients should have that information, but it believed the labeling requirement would increase the cost of blood and lead to an all-volunteer system that would reduce competition among suppliers, commercial as well as nonprofit. It recommended instead that all blood, volunteer as well as commercial, be clearly labeled as to its risk of hepatitis, that commercial suppliers that could demonstrate better than average hepatitis records for their blood be permitted to include that information on the label, and that the National Blood Policy's goal of eliminating all commercial blood be reviewed because more commercialism in blood delivery, under appropriate safeguards, might be the most appropriate way of ensuring adequate supplies of high-quality blood at low prices.

In the end HEW and the bureau rejected the council's proposal, as they did all or part of the recommendations submitted by the National Bureau of Standards and the GAO. Instead, they required labeling of all blood products on the basis of evidence about the likely effects on transfusion-related hepatitis for the system as a whole and ignored situations that were exceptions to the general case. Their concern was to improve the quality of the total system through an estimated threefold reduction in the average rate of transfusion-re-lated hepatitis achievable only by eliminating all paid donors so as to eliminate all commercial sources. They considered the loss of a few high-quality nonprofit paid donor groups unimportant in relation to the general benefit to be achieved, and they were confident of the ability of the volunteer services to replace any lost supply without unusual increases in costs or dislocation of the system. The prag-matism exhibited by HEW and the bureau in this decision is best understood by comparing it with the decision of both agencies about blood derivatives, where a similar situation existed. Neither agency supported labeling requirements for blood derivatives to eliminate commercial sources. Both realized that replacement of the commercial supply of plasma by the voluntary services was not practical. Better a higher risk of hepatitis in an adequate supply of derivatives than a lesser risk in an inadequate supply.

Subsequent events supported the actions of HEW and the bureau. The incidence of transfusion-related hepatitis fell by 40 percent be-tween 1970 and 1977,[10] in part because commercial sources were elim-inated; the lost commercial supply was replaced by increased voluntary supply without serious shortages; and the rate of increase in the cost of blood to the hospitals after the labeling requirement was introduced was only slightly greater than the prior rate.

Altruism, the National Blood Policy and the Bureau of Biologics. Did altruistic considerations significantly affect the formulation by HEW of the National Blood Policy and the decision of the Bureau of Biologics to require the labeling of blood? Did either or both act primarily out of concerns that were neither scientific nor economic but rather supportive of volunteerism for social and ethical reasons? The questions are very difficult to answer. Titmuss's work had a great stimulating and mobilizing effect on many persons in and outside government, persons who felt strongly that commercial trading in human tissue was immoral, that blood—often referred to as "the gift of life"—should not be bartered and sold like a commodity. Others, including business people and economists, took the opposite view: that blood should be treated as a commodity to be bought and sold in markets. The argument was never resolved; it continues, but now it encompasses other human tissue, not solely blood.

130

Information about the deliberations and action of the HEW task force responsible for the National Blood Policy and those of the Bureau of Biologics regarding labeling requirements shows little evidence of altruistic considerations. That such considerations influenced the formulation of the National Blood Policy can be inferred from the explanation following the first policy statement in the document, which encouraged the formation of an all-voluntary system and the elimination of commercialism in the acquisition of whole blood and blood components for transfusion. "The ultimate aims of this policy are improvement in the quality of the supply of blood and blood products and *development of an appropriate ethical climate for the increasing use of human tissues for therapeutic medical purposes.*"[11] Further evidence of altruistic influence can be found in a background paper to the policy, in which the following comment is made regarding the plasma and blood derivatives sector: "It [National Blood Policy] would leave untouched, *for the time being,* the commercial acquisition of plasma and the preparation and marketing of plasma derivatives."[12] Apparently the task force had concerns about commercialism in the blood derivatives sector but concluded that further action would have to await "the acquisition of information on which future policy could be developed."[13]

No evidence is available on the effects, if any, of altruism on the decision of the Bureau of Biologics. The basis for proposing the labeling requirement was clearly reduction of the risk of posttransfusion hepatitis. Analyses of the requirement presented by the various parties to the debate were all couched in cost-benefit terms. Philosophical biases clearly existed in the opposite positions taken by the Council on Wage and Price Stability and HEW, the former clearly favoring retention of commercialism and stimulation of competition while the latter favored an all-volunteer donor system within a regional framework aimed at reducing competition and enhancing cooperation in the delivery of blood services. The National Bureau of Standards and the GAO took a more independent stance, being concerned more with matters of adequate supply while reducing the risks of hepatitis. Little is known of the effects of the bureau's decision on considerations other than those directly related to the hepatitis issue. It appears, then, that considerations of altruism played a role in the development of the National Blood Policy but were of secondary importance to the issue of hepatitis.

Altruism, however, did exert a powerful influence for conversion of many community and regional blood systems from a policy of individual responsibility to one of community responsibility and on the willingness of such systems to accept full responsibility for all blood products and services required by the community or region. Before 1971 and publication of Titmuss's book, blood systems commonly conducted assurance, insurance, and bank credit plans that covered, in varying degrees, the blood needs of members of donor groups and their families. Those who were not covered by such plans had to look to the hospital to supply blood, usually through donations by family and friends to the hospitals, community, or regional replacement plan or through payment of the nonreplacement fee. As proponents and opponents of altruism in blood banking, Titmuss included, have stated, although these assurance and credit plans did not require cash payments, the donors did receive value. Community responsibility, however, envisaged the creation of a relation between the donor and the blood service in which the transfer of value was missing. The community or regional system would assure all persons in the community or region that their blood needs would be met whether or not they belonged to a donor group. All that was required was payment of an amount equal to the costs of recruitment, collection, and processing without replacement or payment of a nonreplacement fee.

In the early 1970s community responsibility became the guiding philosophy of the American Red Cross.[14] In 1972 the Council of Community Blood Centers adopted the philosophy,[15] and some independent community blood centers, members of the American Association of Blood Banks, also did so. Community responsibility is the policy nearest to total altruism. It ensures access for all to whatever blood products they need. In this respect it fulfills part of the accessibility goal of the National Blood Policy, especially when coupled with responsibility for full supply. Without altruistic motivation of donors, it is doubtful that the community responsibility policy could have been successfully implemented.

Motives of the Nonprofit Blood Services.   Were the nonprofit blood services motivated in their efforts to eliminate paid donors primarily by a desire to obtain a competitive advantage over the commercial services? The question is even more difficult to analyze than the question about the role of altruism in the formulation of the National Blood Policy and the introduction of the blood labeling requirement. Unquestionably some community and regional blood services benefited from elimination of their commercial competitors. They no longer had to contend with limited-product-line, limited-service competitors that would not or could not accept responsibility for the full array of needs of the community or region. With the elimination of the commercial services, however, the volunteer services faced the substantial task of replacing the lost supply by expanding their volunteer donor base, a demanding task they could otherwise have avoided. Accepting full responsibility for meeting the blood service needs of a community or region while replacing 10 to 15 percent of the previously existing supply in a relatively short time by expanding volunteer donations hardly seems to be a part of "the 'quiet life' that comes from 'acquir[ing] a monopoly,'" as Tullock and Eckert have suggested.[16] Far easier is the role of the partial blood supplier providing services under an assurance or replacement plan that leaves primary responsibility for meeting total needs to others.

In view of the number of scientists and others not directly involved in blood banking who actively opposed commercial collection, it is hard to believe that self-serving motives of the voluntary blood service managers were the principal reason for elimination of the commercial services. The evidence cited and examined in conjunction with the debate about the risk of hepatitis from commercial blood was largely medical and scientific, not economic or political. Assigning to those who opposed the commercial blood services the principal motive of self-promotion and competitive advantage seems to be unnecessarily ideological and unsupported by the facts.

Recruitment of Voluntary Donors and The Risks of Transfusion-related Disease

Recruiting blood donors through extended voluntary networks as practiced by the American Red Cross and other blood services has been criticized by Eckert for increasing the risks of transfusion-related disease. Eckert's position is that the first-time donor is the main source of risk to the blood recipient; that small, carefully selected and maintained registries of repeat donors would minimize the risk; and that present recruitment methods of the ARC and the other voluntary blood services cast too broad a net and capture too many first-time donors.

Importance of the First-Time Donor. The importance of the repeat donor in minimizing the risks of transfusion-related disease has been established for many years. The position of HEW on this issue was well summarized by the GAO in its study of hepatitis from blood transfusion.

> HEW officials advised us . . . that, if a blood bank collected a large percentage of blood from first-time donors, its [hepatitis B] rate would be higher than that of a blood bank that collected a large percentage from repeat donors. This is because repeat donors would have been previously screened and those testing positive for [hepatitis B] would have been eliminated from the donor population.[17]

In its filing before the Bureau of Biologics in 1975 in the matter of the required labeling of blood, the Council on Wage and Price Stability included a recommendation that reflected the importance of repeat donations in minimizing risks.

> Competition between suppliers, both commercial as well as nonprofit, together with basic regulations of quality and testing procedure, should be encouraged. Organizations could then solicit donors in any lawful manner and would assure quality by extensive and expensive testing and/or careful selection of donors who are monitored for disease and *encouraged to donate repeatedly*.[18]

The lower risk of transfusion-related disease from repeat donors has been shown more precisely in various scientific studies. Dodd, Nath, Bastiaans, and Barker, in their article on hepatitis-associated markers in the American Red Cross donor population, found evidence of the importance of the repeat donor.[19] Using the HBsAg test for detecting the presence of hepatitis B, the authors found incidence rates of HBsAg among first-time donors to the ARC in 1977 and 1978 of 2.16 and 1.99 per 1,000 respectively, while the rates among ARC repeat donors for the same two years were 0.49 and 0.42 per 1,000. Thus, among the donors studied, first-time donors were four times as likely as repeat donors to carry the hepatitis B antigen. Authors of similar studies have reported much the same findings.

It seems reasonable, therefore, to conclude that the first-time donor is the principal source of risk and that efforts should be made to select first-time donors as carefully as possible, to screen them thoroughly with the most effective tests available, and to maintain careful and complete records that associate transfusion-related disease in recipients with the donors from whom the suspect blood was drawn. It is also apparent that, given the present incidence of hepatitis NANB among blood recipients whose transfused blood has been effectively tested for hepatitis B, an effective test for hepatitis B is not necessarily an effective test for other transfusion-related diseases. Therefore, the selection of first-time donors should be based on additional criteria.

The Role of Socioeconomic Status. That socioeconomic status plays an important role in determining the risks of transfusion-related disease among blood donors has been recognized for many years. Objections to commercial donors were based on this association: that those who sold their blood to the commercial services were from lower socioeconomic classes in which the incidence of hepatitis was much higher than in the population as a whole and the need for money was great. Among volunteer donors a similar association has been found by various investigators. In its study of the incidence of HBsAg-positive rates among donor groups, the GAO reported, "Our statistical analysis of the data shows that the socioeconomic conditions of the area from which the donors came was more strongly related to the HBsAg-positive rates than was the factor of whether or not they volunteered or were paid."[20]

In a more recent study by Aach, Szmuness, and others of the incidence of NANB among 1,513 blood recipients at four medical centers in St. Louis, New York, Los Angeles, and Houston, the authors found the differences in NANB attack rates among recipients to be associated in part with differences in the socioeconomic status of the blood donors.[21] In St. Louis, where the attack rate was 4 percent, blood came exclusively from voluntary donations to a community agency; in Houston, where the rate was 18 percent, blood was obtained through a county hospital program, donors to which were principally family and friends of the lower socioeconomic patients served by the hospital. The authors stated:

> The source of donor blood is another variable that has been shown to influence the risk of posttransfusion hepatitis in previous studies as well as this one. This risk is almost certainly due to the inverse relationship between socioeconomic status and rate of infection with hepatitis virus.[22]

Dodd, Nath, Bastiaans, and Barker found marked differences in HBsAg prevalence among first-time ARC donors, depending on the region of the country from which they came and the type of donor group (workplace, military, school, community group, or general community) to which they belonged.[23] Incidence rates among the five donor subpopulations ranged from 3.3 per 1,000 for workplace groups to 1.0 per 1,000 for schools, with an average rate of 2.1 per 1,000 for all groups. In a study of elevated ALT levels (evidencing the presence of NANB hepatitis) among ARC donors, Sherman, Dodd, and others reported significant regional variations in the disease among donors but failed to find an association between elevated ALT levels and several socioeconomic factors, including family income and education. As the authors stated, however, "This lack of association may reflect either the socioeconomic homogeneity of the (ARC) volunteer donor population or the nonspecificity of the test for the actual infectivity of the donor."[24]

Most available evidence suggests that the incidence of transfusion-related hepatitis is substantially different among various groups in the population; that region, type of donor group, and socioeconomic status of donors are significant characteristics in assessing probable transfusion-related risks, especially for first-time donors; and that

135

attention should be given to these factors in planning donor recruit-ment and blood collections. Regional variations, of course, cannot be controlled, for most transfused blood must be collected in the same region. The other two factors, however, do vary within regions and can be considered in forming and selecting donor groups.

For AIDS the association between the type of group to which a potential donor belongs and the incidence of the disease is more specific and pronounced. Those at greatest risk fall into three cate-gories: homosexuals, drug abusers, and Haitian immigrants. The last two categories are rather easily avoided in forming donor groups. Homosexuals, however, are found in almost all socioeconomic strata and types of donor groups. Avoiding the formation of groups in which there are likely to be homosexuals is impossible because many hom-osexuals are not known to be homosexuals. Consequently, selective formation of donor groups is a weak means of avoiding the risk of disease from donations from this subpopulation. Better is the present practice of widespread dissemination of information on the associa-tion of AIDS in blood recipients with donations by high-risk homo-sexuals, coupled with appeals to homosexuals to refrain from blood donation and to inform the blood service to remove the suspect unit if they do donate blood.

The American Red Cross and Donor Group Formation. Evidence previously cited shows that an emphasis on repeat donors and attention to the type of affinity group and socioeconomic status of first-time donors are important in minimizing transfusion-related disease risks. Eckert suggests that the ARC, because of its emphasis on volunteers, has been indiscriminate in recruiting first-time donors and has insufficiently emphasized the use of repeat donors. He implies that as a result the risks of transfusion-related hepatitis and AIDS from ARC blood are unnecessarily high and could be significantly reduced by the use of carefully selected registries of paid repeat donors. What evidence is there to support his contention? Almost the only fact available on this subject is that ARC donors give an average of 1.5 times per year whereas the maximum number of yearly donations is 5.[25] Obviously ARC donors give blood far less frequently than they could. This should not be interpreted, however, as evidence of a disproportionate number of first-time donors among them. Many repeat donors donate only once a year.

A more definitive answer to the question of the use of repeat donors in the ARC donor pool can be inferred from results of the study by Dodd, Nath, Bastiaans, and Barker.[26] The authors found that since 1974 the detection rate of HBsAg among ARC donors has declined from 1.25 per 1,000 to 0.66 per 1,000, where it stabilized in

1979. By 1979 the incidence of HBsAg-positive tests among first-time ARC donors was 2.1 per 1,000, whereas the incidence among repeat donors was 0.40 per 1,000. That the positive test rate for all ARC donors (0.66 per 1,000) was much closer to the rate for repeat donors than to the rate for first-time donors is evidence that the entire ARC donor population must contain a predominance of repeat donors.[27]

This predominance is not surprising given the methods of recruitment practiced by ARC, which for reasons of efficiency has emphasized mobile collections from large groups, where the number of units collected would be the greatest for the effort made. These large donor groups are locally managed by volunteers who, in cooperation with professional recruiters from the ARC, maintain lists of previous donors, who are called and urged to participate in annual or biannual collections. The result is a relatively large pool of donors repeating at rates less frequent than the maximum; nonetheless, they are repeat donors.

These observations do not mean that present methods of donor recruitment practiced by the ARC and other voluntary blood services could not be improved. The importance of the repeat donor needs to be emphasized. This message should be conveyed to the various donor groups so that they will better understand why frequent donations are so important. It also needs to be conveyed to individual donors, especially those who press the ARC and other voluntary blood services to maximize the number of blood donors. Such a policy may appeal to certain instincts of equality among donors and recruiters, but it is contrary to the aim of minimizing transfusion-related disease. Finally, the importance of socioeconomic status in determining the incidence of hepatitis and other transfusion-related diseases needs to be understood and used in establishing new donor groups. It also needs to be understood by those critics who complain that the voluntary services make insufficient efforts to penetrate the poorer strata of the urban population. The aim of efficiency that led the voluntary blood services to emphasize recruitment from easily accessible middle-class organizations and donor groups and from previous donors has worked to the benefit of the blood system as a whole, for these are the donors who should be solicited to minimize the risks of transfusion-related disease.

Paid Donors, the Commercial Blood Services, and Transfusion-related Disease

Would the reentry of paid donors and the commercial services into the blood products sector in the form of selected registries of cash donors reduce the incidence of transfusion-related disease? Eckert cites the experiences of the Mayo clinic and the Massachusetts General Hospital in the 1970s as evidence that such a change in blood policy would lower the disease rate and increase competition. There are several reasons to doubt this outcome, however, reasons that lend support to the present policy.

First, the experiences of the Mayo clinic and the Massachusetts General Hospital were not representative of the experience of non-profit hospitals with paid donors during the 1970s. The two organizations obviously took unusual care in selecting and maintaining their paid donor panels. For Mayo an important factor in producing such a low incidence of transfusion-associated disease appears to have been the socioeconomic characteristics of the subpopulation and region from which the donors were drawn. Prior experience provides no evidence to support the contention that nonprofit hospitals as a whole could develop and maintain similar low-risk groups. Quite the contrary, evidence from the 1970s indicates that the nonprofit hospitals that maintained paid donor groups had transfusion-related disease rates twice as high as those of the voluntary groups. There appears to be no reason to suppose that under the present conditions, with the cost-cutting pressures produced by the introduction of DRGs, the nonprofit hospitals would be any more successful than they were in the 1970s.

Second, the record of the commercial services in the 1970s was the worst of all. Paid commercial donors consistently had rates of transfusion-related hepatitis three to five times those of the voluntary groups. There were exceptions, but they were few. Of course, it is possible to speculate that with sufficient monetary incentive commercial services could afford to pay whatever was necessary to recruit sufficient numbers of donors to make reentry possible. To do so, however, they would have to concentrate recruitment on those subpopulations where the incidence of transfusion-related disease is low—in middle-class institutions such as schools, colleges, clubs, and churches. That would not be easy, would probably be expensive, and would be unlikely to yield an appreciable increment to the present supply. Moreover, attempts by the commercial services to penetrate the middle class to form registries of low-risk paid donors would disrupt many present relations between the middle-class groups and the voluntary services and would probably lead to an increase in recruitment costs.

Third, the use of paid donors willing to donate repeatedly, at least four to five times a year, would not necessarily significantly reduce transfusion-related disease. ARC donors as a group exhibit HBsAg-positive test rates quite close to those of repeat donors. Such donors, however, do not donate nearly as often as four or five times a year. There is no evidence of a significant relation between the number of donations per year and the risk of transfusion-related disease. Whether or not a person is a repeat donor is the important determinant of the associated disease risk.

Fourth, in view of the present state of the blood products market, in which the demand for whole blood and red cells has leveled off and capacity is more than sufficient to meet demand, it is difficult to see why a commercial service intending to provide a high-quality product would enter the market. The disappearance of growth in demand for whole blood and red cells, which are the volume products and the ones that carry the highest margins, means that financial success would have to be secured by taking absolute sales as well as market share away from the voluntary services. This would have to be accomplished in a market where existing competitors are now well positioned, price competition is growing, and excess capacity is growing. Unless an enterprise has a unique advantage over organizations already in such a market, there would be little rational incentive for it to enter. Most commercial services appear to have no such unique advantage and therefore no reason to enter this market.

If the commercial services were permitted to reenter the market, those that did would more likely adopt a low-cost, limited-service strategy and concentrate on the large urban markets. Under the DRG system hospitals have strong incentive to reduce costs. The availability of a low-cost commerical supplier in a community or region would be attractive to some hospitals as it was in the 1970s. To be the low-cost supplier in such a market, however, the commercial service would have to keep its costs of blood procurement below those of the voluntary services. Moreover, it would be under further pressure to reduce costs to match or exceed any reductions the voluntary services were able to achieve through their current efforts to improve efficiency. Such pressure on procurement costs is inconsistent with developing and maintaining registries of high-quality paid donors. The commercial services would be more likely to accept whatever donors met the minimum test requirements imposed by law and were willing to donate for relatively small cash payments. Such donors would most likely come from those socioeconomic groups where the incidence of undetectable NANB and AIDS is highest. Schools and colleges from which low-risk middle-class donors willing to sell blood for small cash payments might be drawn do not appear to be a sufficiently large source to meet the requirements of the commercial services.

While direct evidence is scarce, there is little evidence that permitting the reentry of paid donors and the commercial services into the blood products market would significantly increase the high-quality supply, and therefore, significantly reduce the rate of transfusion-related disease. The conditions under which a few paid donor groups have shown low rates of transfusion-related disease were unusual and not readily replicated; the commercial services have never shown an ability to provide substantial quantities of high-quality blood; and present competitive conditions in the blood products market are such that entry by commercial enterprises intent on providing a high-quality product at reasonable cost is simply not attractive. What is more likely to occur if commerical services are permitted to reenter the market is a repetition of the events of the 1970s: paid commercial blood would become the low-cost supply drawn from higher-risk subpopulations willing to sell their blood at prices low enough to permit commercial producers to make a profit in selected small niches of the blood products market.

Notes

1. Garrott Allen, "Post-Transfusion Hepatitis," *California Medical Journal*, April 1966; Norman Boeve, Loren Winterscheid, and Alvin Merendion, "Fibrinogen-transmitted Hepatitis in the Surgical Patient," *Annals of Surgery*, vol. 170 (1969), pp. 833–38; and Stephen Cohen and William Dougherty, "Transfusion Hepatitis Arising from Addict Blood Donors," *Journal of the American Medical Association*, vol. 203 (1968), p. 427.

2. Garrott Allen, "Immunization against Serum Hepatitis from Blood Transfusion," *Annals of Surgery*, October 1966; and National Communicable Disease Center, *Hepatitis Surveillance*, September 1967.

3. John Walsh, Robert Purcell, Andrew Morrow, et al., "Post-Transfusion Hepatitis after Open Heart Operations," *Journal of the American Medical Association*, vol. 211 (1970), pp. 261–65.

4. Reported in U.S. Comptroller General, *Hepatitis from Blood Transfusions: Evaluation of Methods to Reduce the Problem*, U.S. General Accounting Office, February 1976.

5. "National Blood Policy," *Federal Register*, vol. 39, no. 176 (1974), p. 32709.

6. National Bureau of Standards, *Cost Analysis of Blood Banking Alternatives*, U.S. Department of Commerce, NBS Technical Note 777, September 1973; U.S. Department of Health, Education, and Welfare, *Post-Transfusion Hepatitis: Cases, Deaths and Costs*, 1973; and U.S. Comptroller General, *Hepatitis from Blood Transfusions*.

7. *Comments of the Department of Health, Education and Welfare on the Comptroller General's Report to the Congress of the United States*, entitled "Hepatitis Resulting from the Transfusion of Blood—An Evaluation of Four Methods to Reduce the Problem," October 10, 1975.

8. Reuben Kessel, "Transfused Blood, Serum Hepatitis, and the Coase Theorem," *Journal of Law and Economics*, vol. 17, no. 2 (October 1974).

9. Council on Wage and Price Stability, *Whole Blood and Red Cells*, Docket No. 75N-0316, January 1976.

10. Personal communication from Roger Dodd, American Red Cross, September 1984.

11. "National Blood Policy," *Federal Register*, vol. 39, no. 47 (1974), p. 9329 (italics added).

12.   Office of Special Health Projects, HEW, *Background Information on National Blood Policy*, July 1973 (italics added).

13.   Ibid.

14.   The philosophy was first expressed by the American Red Cross in Board of Governors, *Essential Features of a National Blood Service*, February 22, 1972; reproduced in National Heart and Lung Institute, *Summary Report: NHLI's Blood Resources Studies*, Department of Health, Education, and Welfare, 1972.

15.   Communication from Jane Starke, Council of Community Blood Centers, September 1984.

16.   Gordon Tullock, "Commentary," in David Johnson, ed., *Blood Policy: Issues and Alternatives* (Washington, D.C.: American Enterprise Institute 1977), p. 154.

17.   U.S. Comptroller General, *Hepatitis from Blood Transfusions*.

18.   Council on Wage and Price Stability, *Whole Blood and Red Cells* (italics added).

19.   Roger Dodd, Nrapendra Nath, Mary Jane Bastiaans, and Lewellys Barker, "Hepatitis Associated Markers in the American Red Cross Donor Population: Ten Years' Experience," *Vox Sanguis* (1982), pp. 203–10.

20.   U.S. Comptroller General, *Hepatitis from Blood Transfusions*.

21.   Richard Aach, Wolf Szmuness, James Mosely, Blaine Hollinger, Richard Kahn, Gladd Stevens, Virginia Edwards, and Jochewed Werch, "Serum Alanine Aminotransferase of Donors in Relation to the Risk of Non-A, Non-B Hepatitis in Recipients," *New England Journal of Medicine*, April 23, 1981.

22.   Ibid, p. 992.

23.   Dodd, et al., "Hepatitis Associated Markers."

24.   Kenneth Sherman, Roger Dodd, and the American Red Cross Alanine Aminotransferase Study Group, "Alanine Aminotransferase Levels among Volunteer Blood Donors: Geographic Variations and Risk Factors," *Journal of Infectious Diseases*, vol. 145, no. 3 (March 1982), p. 386.

25.   Letter from American Red Cross, August 1984.

26.   Dodd, et al., "Hepatitis Associated Markers."

27.   From these statistics it is possible to estimate that 85 percent of ARC donors are repeat donors; that is:

$$0.40X + 2.1(1-X) = 0.66$$
$$1.7X = 1.44$$
$$X = 0.85$$

4

Regionalism, Conflicting Philosophies, and Competition

Competition in blood products was subdued and confined largely to noneconomic considerations during the 1970s. It was a period of enormous growth, particularly for regional and community blood services, growth occasioned principally by rapidly expanding demands for an ever-increasing array of products and services. As a consequence most regional and community blood services were engrossed in meeting demands within their service areas and gave little attention to other opportunities for expansion.

Competitive behavior centered on three noneconomic issues: (1) the quality of blood from commercial sources; (2) the preferred form of organization for an expanding blood services system; and (3) philosophies concerning the obligation of blood recipients. The issue of quality and its competitive implications was discussed in chapter 2. Differences over the preferred form of organization centered on regionalism, an organizational form strongly supported by the National Blood Policy and encouraged, developed, and implemented by the American Blood Commission. Conflicting philosophies about the obligation of blood recipients formed the basis for continuing disputes over issues such as the nonreplacement fee, tax credits for blood donations, and participation of the American Red Cross (ARC) in the National Clearinghouse Program.

Most of the competitive interplay among nonprofit blood services arose from differences over the preferred form of organization and conflicting philosophies. The ARC, and to a lesser extent the newly formed Council of Community Blood Centers (CCBC), supported regionalism and community responsibility while the American Association of Blood Banks (AABB), representing principally the hospital blood banks, opposed certain aspects of regionalism and advocated individual responsibility. Most of what Eckert views as monopolistic behavior by the ARC during this period was motivated by differences on these issues, particularly differences in philosophy. Whether the

ARC achieved any competitive advantage over members of the AABB as a result of its stands on these issues is difficult to determine. What is clear, however, is that its actions sprang from noneconomic considerations: an endeavor to cooperate with the federal government in its effort to develop a nationwide blood system and philosophical differences with the AABB about the obligations of blood recipients.

Effects of Regionalism

"Regionalism" is a term used in blood banking for the organizational form designed to produce and distribute the full range of blood products and services required for hospitals within a large geographic area to practice modern blood therapy. A community blood center is similar to a region in the array of products and services it provides but generally serves a smaller area. Both forms may be governed by a single management or by a coordinated management drawn from associated community and hospital blood services. The regional form has been employed in blood services since the 1940s. Its attractiveness to the federal government predates the National Blood Policy; it is the form specified in most federal health initiatives, beginning with the Regional Medical Program and the Comprehensive Health Planning Agencies of the 1960s and continuing throughout the 1970s in such programs as the Health Systems Agencies. The encouragement and support given regionalism in the National Blood Policy and efforts to implement it through the American Blood Commission reflected a federal conviction that it was the most effective way to organize a national blood system. Size was an important consideration in the support for regionalism, for size measured in population served was needed to provide both support for effective recruitment of voluntary blood donors and the demand needed to justify the array of products and services associated with a full-service region.

Events Leading to the National Blood Policy.   In 1972 the National Heart and Lung Institute (NHLI) elicited statements from the two major blood services organizations, the ARC and the AABB, of their positions on its exploratory efforts to form a nationwide blood system. The position paper issued by the ARC board of governors, *Essential Features of a National Blood Service*, included the following statements:

1. Whole blood and blood components for transfusion should be available to all who need them and preferably should come from voluntary donors.

2. The only charge made for blood or its components should be related to the cost of collection, processing, and distribution.

3. There should be a voluntary, nationwide, nonprofit service with uniform standards of operation—medical, technical and ' administrative. . . .

4. Pre-established eligibility requirements through individual or group credits, and penalty replacement fees, should be eliminated.

That statement ended: "The Red Cross is prepared to join with government and with voluntary organizations to work for the future attainment of these essential features."[1].

The statement was issued in response to the NHLI's interest in determining the ARC's position on a nationwide blood system. Viewed in full, it is clearly an expression of cooperative intent rather than of monopolistic aim.

At the same time the American Association of Blood Banks issued a statement of its position on a nationwide blood system. It reaffirmed its support for the goal of a wholly voluntary blood supply, proposed a time schedule for its members to achieve the goal of collecting 100 percent voluntary blood, reaffirmed its support for the nonreplacement fee as a necessary tool for recruiting donors and urged the formation of a commission consisting of representatives of the ARC, the AABB, and medical, hospital, and consumer organizations "to improve national coordination of blood bank systems and programs."[2]

Comparison of the positions of the two organizations shows the bases for their future differences:

- The ARC fully supported the development of a nationwide blood system; the AABB supported the formation of a commission to improve national coordination of blood bank systems and programs.
- The ARC supported the elimination of individual and group credits as a basis for blood eligibility and opposed the nonreplacement fee; the AABB strongly supported the concept of individual responsibility and continued use of the fee.

Differences in the positions of the two organizations sprang from differences in their forms and functions and in their size and methods of operation. The ARC was a single organization with fifty-nine regions functioning under a central management that set overall policies. The AABB was a trade association representing its membership, which consisted of over 1,300 voting organizations, principally hospital blood banks, many of which collected and processed blood. The ARC was in a position to become directly involved in the creation and conduct of a national blood system, for its regional form of organization fitted the model envisaged by the government. The AABB, as a trade association rather than an operating system, was not in a position to participate directly; moreover, the organizational form of the majority of its members did not fit the government's model. Hospital blood banks were generally too small to be effective collectors and distributors in a growing national system; therefore, they correctly perceived the creation of a national system based on regionalism as a threat to their continued existence. Thus the ARC and the AABB were bound to clash over regionalism.

Decline of Hospital Blood Banks. Subsequent events confirmed the wary position of the AABB. Although a single national system never came into being, the regional and community forms of organization predominated in the growth of blood services during the 1970s. In 1971 some 800 hospital blood banks collected 1.6 million units of whole blood; in 1980 over 1,660 hospital blood banks collected 1.1 million units—a decrease in units collected of approximately 33 percent despite an increase in collecting hospitals of over 100 percent.[3] Regional and community blood services had taken over a substantial portion of the supply previously collected by hospitals and also provided the entire increase in supply between the two years. By 1980 hospitals that continued to collect blood did so largely to supplement the supply provided by their regional or community blood programs.

Why did the hospitals retreat from their 1971 position as substantial collectors of whole blood? Part of the reason lies in the elimination of the paid donor, the most reliable source of blood for many hospitals. Part lies in the ever-increasing array of blood products and services required by physicians and surgeons, an array only the very largest hospital blood banks were able to provide. And part lies in the hospitals' incentives to abandon a task most were ill fitted to undertake. The average processing fee paid by the hospitals to regional or community blood centers was less than the cost to the hospitals of collecting blood.[4] Moreover, the fee was passed along to the patient, who could transfer part of it to a third party. Therefore, hospital costs were not adversely affected by the substitution of sources. Only the nonreplacement fee was lost; for most hospitals this was insufficient incentive to continue collecting their needed supply of whole blood. Hospitals whose regional or community services were unable to meet all their needs and hospitals that had ready access to replacement donors continued to collect blood as supplementary suppliers. But by 1980 almost 90 percent of the nation's blood needs were provided by regional and community blood services.[5]

To what extent did the American Red Cross gain competitively from the extensive growth in regional and community blood services of the 1970s? Two measures are readily available. First, the number of ARC regional blood centers declined from fifty-nine in 1971 to fifty-seven in 1980. Second, the ARC's share of total blood collections rose from 39.5 percent in 1971 to 50 percent in 1980, an increase of 10.5 percentage points, which returned the system to the 50 percent share it held in 1963. Undoubtedly, the regionalism of the 1970s was beneficial to the ARC, as it was to other regional and community blood systems, but not to the extent that the ARC attained a near monopoly over blood services in the United States.

The Consequences of Philosophical Differences

Of greater importance than the upsurge in regionalism and its effects on hospital blood banks were the different philosophies of the ARC and the AABB about the obligation of blood recipients. The AABB believed in strict individual responsibility; blood recipients were expected to replace blood transfused in some ratio ranging from 1:1 to 3:1 and to pay a nonreplacement fee in addition to the processing fee for any blood not replaced. The ARC held to the philosophy of community responsibility under which the community, not the individual, was considered responsible for meeting the blood needs of all patients and the regional or community blood system for mobilizing the community to meet those needs. That was also the philosophy of the Council of Community Blood Centers, whose members split from the AABB, partly over this issue, in 1971.

The Nonreplacement Fee.   Philosophical difference was the basis for the continuing dispute over use of the nonreplacement fee. The AABB insisted the fee was needed by some of its members to motivate donors—almost always relatives and friends of the blood recipient. Recipients sufficiently well-to-do to pay the replacement fee were relieved of their obligation to replace the blood. The ARC saw the fee as a disavowal of community responsibility.

One major difference between the two organizations lay in the ability of their member organizations to recruit voluntary donors. Hospital blood banks for the most part had limited abilities in this respect. The nonreplacement fee presumably compensated them for the difficulties they encountered in replacing blood. Since the hospitals also charged a processing fee to cover the cost of obtaining the blood, the nonreplacement fee was an added revenue source. Regional and community blood centers following the community responsibility philosophy could recover all costs of recruiting donors and collecting and processing blood through the processing fee that they charged to the hospitals for blood.

146

Thus the disagreement of the ARC and the AABB over use of the nonreplacement fee stemmed primarily from different philosophies motivated by different abilities to recruit donors, as well as from a desire by the ARC to adhere to a stricter altruism. Although the disagreement may have had economic consequences, the aim of the ARC was certainly not monopoly.

Tax Credits. The ARC's continuing opposition to tax credits for blood donors and the AABB's support of them were also based on differences in philosophy. The ARC viewed tax credits as a form of direct compensation of donors, the equivalent of cash payments.[6] The AABB viewed them as another means of motivating voluntary donors and considered their cash equivalence unimportant. It emphasized the stimulative effect such credits could have on blood donation at a time when supply in many areas was expected to fall short of demand.

Again the dispute reflected deep-seated philosophical differences arising from differences in operations and aims. The loss of tax credits undoubtedly had a greater effect on hospital blood banks than on regional and community blood centers, which by the late 1970s had demonstrated their ability to recruit voluntary donors in sufficient numbers to compensate for the lost commercial supply and decreases in hospital collections.

The Clearinghouse Controversy. The differences between the AABB and the ARC culminated in 1976 in their dispute over the ARC's decision to withdraw from the National Clearinghouse Program (NCP) of the AABB. The NCP was formed in 1951 to facilitate the exchange of blood credits and blood among participating members when participants in one service were transfused with blood provided by another. Periodically, monetary payments were exchanged between services to settle outstanding balances.

The ARC began to participate in the NCP in 1961 and continued to do so until 1976. From 1972 on, however, differences in philosophies and operating methods created ever-increasing problems. By 1976 the ARC, along with United Blood Services and the Greater New York Blood Program, decided to withdraw from the system.

In its letter of withdrawal the ARC stated the principal reasons for its decision.

- The NCP was based on the philosophy of individual responsibility of the blood recipient to replace the transfused blood or to pay a nonreplacement fee, both of which were contrary to the community responsibility philosophy of the ARC.
- Continued membership in the NCP of commercial blood banks,

to which the ARC was obligated at times to ship voluntary blood and which sold that blood, was contrary to ARC's policies.
- Because of the community responsibility philosophy, ARC regions participating in the NCP were at a disadvantage in the exchange of credits or blood with non-ARC services that followed the individual responsibility philosophy.[7]

Other technical objections were voiced by the ARC, but they were obviously of lesser importance. In lieu of participation of the NCP, the ARC proposed a facility-to-facility program whereby it would ship blood to non-ARC hospitals that transfused ARC participants and cooperate with patients from AABB communities on the same basis— in brief, no NCP participation, no blood credits, no monetary payments, only the exchange of voluntary blood.

This action had serious monetary consequences for the AABB and its members which had benefited from the NCP arrangement in two ways. First, AABB members, stressing individual responsibility, kept careful records of the blood credits due them from ARC regions while ARC regions kept much poorer records of blood due from AABB services. As a consequence ARC regions were generally net debtors and had either to ship blood to AABB members in whatever multiple of the transfused units was established as the replacement equivalent or pay the nonreplacement fee, which averaged $35 per unit. By withdrawing from the NCP, ARC regions reduced their indebtedness to AABB members to the number of units of blood actually transfused to ARC participants. Second, participation in the NCP required payment of a handling fee of about $3 per unit, which went directly to the AABB as compensation for costs it incurred in operating the NCP. By withdrawing from the NCP, the ARC saved approximately $300,000 per year in such fees.

Although harsh remarks were exchanged between the two organizations after the ARC withdrew from the NCP, in time the two organizations worked out parallel systems for exchanging blood among members of their systems. Members of the two organizations still exchange blood, largely through individual agreements. By 1981 growing blood inventories in the two systems and reduced losses and outdated units had substantially lessened the need for a single exchange system. This was one reason for the failure of the effort by the ABC in 1982–1983 to draw the AABB, the ARC, and the CCBC together as participants in a new national system to facilitate the shipment of blood from surplus to deficit regions. A second reason was the concern about antitrust implications on the part of the ARC and of the American Blood Resources Association, which objected to the proposed agreement on the grounds that it would exclude commercial members from participation.[8]

A review of the history of this dispute between the ARC and the AABB during the 1970s finds little evidence to support Eckert's contention that the ARC withdrew from the NCP to further its monopolistic aims. A more pausible explanation is that the roots of the dispute lay in the contradictory philosophies of the two organizations and their inability to compromise.

Conclusion

Careful examination of the evidence about developments in the nation's blood system during the past decade has failed to substantiate Eckert's contention that the Department of Health, Education, and Welfare made a serious error when it acted to exclude paid donors-from the blood products sector in the 1970s. By eliminating the paid donor, the department succeeded in eliminating the principal source of transfusion-related hepatitis B, the commercial blood service. Eckert is correct that the first-time blood donor is the main source of continuing risk of transfusion-related disease, particularly non-A, non-B hepatitis, an opinion shared by blood bankers and the government. It does not follow, however, that the American Red Cross and other voluntary blood services have been indiscriminate in recruiting donors. Since repeat donors constitute approximately 85 percent of the ARC total, the risk of transfusion-related disease associable with the entire ARC donor population is very close to the risk associable with a population exclusively of repeat donors. The ARC's methods of recruiting voluntary donors emphasize regular visits to primarily middle-class groups most of whose members have previously donated.

Similarly the evidence does not support Eckert's contention that the opposition of the ARC to the nonreplacement fee and to tax credits for blood donation and its withdrawal from the National Clearinghouse Program were forms of covert monopolistic behavior. They arose from continuing philosophical differences with the AABB over community versus individual responsibility. To one trained to think in economic terms, such a controversy may be hard to comprehend, but the differences exist, the positions of both parties have been firmly held, and they have affected the behavior of the organizations in many ways.

The ARC did not seek to monopolize a voluntary, nationwide blood system. The ARC's board of governors specifically stated its willingness to cooperate with the government and other voluntary agencies in forming such a system. Neither the present market position, nor the market behavior of the ARC constitutes a near monopoly. Consequently, any recommendation that the ARC be required to divest itself of its regional blood system is supported only by the argument that the conduct of its operations is not in strict accord with the letter of its charter of 1905. This is weak reasoning, for if all organizations were required to adhere to the strictest interpretations of their original charters, a cataclysmic upheaval would take place in social and economic activity. Such a proposal would be unnecessarily destructive of an effective regional blood service system now serving the interests of the American people.

The idea of encouraging the reentry into the blood products system of commercial services with panels of selected cash donors to reduce the risks of AIDS and non-A, non-B hepatitis carries considerable risk. Present economic conditions in the blood products market are such that new commercial entrants would find it most difficult to achieve a satisfactory return on their investment while offering a high-quality service. The demand for whole blood and red cells, the principal products driving the market, is leveling off while the capacity to supply blood is still rising, so that excess supplies are appearing in a number of regions. This condition, together with the strong market position now held by regional and community blood centers, provides little financial incentive for the reentry of commercial firms, particularly those intent on providing a quality superior to that offered by the voluntary services. To achieve such high quality, commercial firms would have to draw most of their blood from members of socioeconomic groups for whom cash payments have the least appeal. They would thus incur unusually high costs of recruitment, which would hardly be conducive to achieving a satisfactory return on investment.

What is more likely is that commercial firms would serve the low-price market niche, a niche that is sure to grow under the pressure of DRGs. To be successful in this part of the market, a firm must offer low prices by keeping down its costs of recruitment. The easiest way of doing so is to recruit donors from those socioeconomic groups most in need of cash, using as the sole test of quality the ability of donors to pass minimum legally required tests for blood quality. Since neither AIDS nor non-A, non-B hepatitis can be detected by present testing procedures and the risks of hepatitis are greatest in those groups most in need of funds, the outcome of Eckert's proposals would most likely be a repetition of the problems of the 1960s and 1970s—excessive risk of disease from commercial sources.

If we reject the solutions proposed by Eckert, what can be done to reduce the risks of transfusion-related disease? The outlook for development of a test to detect the AIDS virus or viruses in blood is reasonably good. In the meantime indirect screening of donors through private questionnaires or other means for donors to notify their blood service of excessive risk appear to be the most effective procedure. For non-A, non-B hepatitis, the more serious threat to blood recipients, the best practice is for the voluntary blood services to use care in selecting donors by concentrating recruitment on groups known to have the lowest risk of hepatitis and maximizing the number of repeat donations from those groups. The voluntary services should not be influenced by advocates of recruiting the greatest possible number of voluntary donors. Although such a policy might appear fair and reasonable, it is a high-risk policy that must be avoided.

How can price and cost increases in blood services be restrained and efficiency be increased? A significant trend that may help is the leveling off of demand for whole blood and red cells, which accounted for 75 percent of the increases in total revenues of regional and community blood services over the past decade. As the demand levels off, the opportunity for offsetting cost increases by increases in red cell prices will diminish. If blood services are to continue to prosper under these changing conditions, their managers must either look to new products for growth or find ways of improving efficiency. Although the demands for platelets and for fresh-frozen plasma have grown appreciably in recent years and may well continue to grow—particularly the demand for platelets—added revenues from these sources are likely to be far less than those previously obtained from increased prices and volumes of red cells.

Hospitals, hospital chains, and hospital buying groups are all beginning to look for ways of reducing their costs. Reduced prices of blood, particularly of red cells, are a way of accomplishing this. As excess supplies of red cells appear in some regions, many blood service managers will want to distribute them to large users in regions where prices are high. This form of competition is likely to create appreciable economic pressure on blood prices, particularly in high-priced regions, which should be an added inducement for managers in those regions to seek new ways of improving their operating efficiency. This competitive trend is also likely to bring pressure to bear on blood services to unbundle their product and service prices and to shift some of the revenue burden from red cells, which have borne the brunt, to other products and services, which, if charged for at all, have been priced at marginal cost.

Blood services managers facing the greatest price competition and pressure on costs are most likely to seek more efficient ways of operating. Because others may be less inclined to do so, other methods of inducing change are needed. One important opportunity is to increase markedly the information provided by blood services about their operations. Like most nonprofit organizations, blood services usually release minimum financial and operating information to the public. Their secrecy is caused by competitive behavior as intense among nonprofit as among for-profit organizations, by fear of criticism from the press and the public, and by internal information systems incapable of providing needed information even if the organization were inclined to release it. A major improvement in the conduct of nonprofit activities could be achieved by requiring all nonprofit service operations to disclose annually detailed information on their prices, costs, and operating and financial performance. Such information would allow local organizations served to judge the reasonableness of prices charged and costs incurred in relation to those of similar services throughout the country. This was one of the original purposes of the National Blood Policy, a purpose that was lost sight of in the great expansion era of the 1970s but that needs reinvigoration in the cost-conscious atmosphere of the 1980s. If hospitals, hospital chains, and hospital buying groups could compare prices and costs of their current suppliers with those of other suppliers, they could press for needed reform where warranted or seek out alternative sources of supply. In view of the dominance of nonprofit regional and community blood services in the blood products market and the likelihood that their dominance will continue, full disclosure of operating and financial information appears to be one sure route to constraining prices and costs and improving efficiency.

Notes

1. Statement by American National Red Cross Board of Governors, dated February 22, 1972; reprinted in National Heart and Lung Institute, *Summary Report: NHLI's Blood Resources Studies*, Department of Health, Education, and Welfare, 1972.

2. *AABB Position Statement*, adopted by AABB Executive Committee, February 8, 1972, and approved by AABB Board of Directors, March 16, 1972; reprinted in NHLI, *Summary Report*.

3. NHLI, *Summary Report*; and Douglas Surgenor and Sarah Schnitzer, *The Nation's Blood Resource 1979 and 1980* (Report submitted to Division of Blood Diseases and Resources, National Heart, Lung, and Blood Institute, 1983; scheduled for publication in 1984).

4. Edward Wallace and Mary Ann Wallace, *Hospital Transfusion Charges and Community Blood Center Costs* (Report submitted to Division of Blood Diseases and Resources, National Heart, Lung, and Blood Institute, 1984; forthcoming).

5. Surgenor and Schnitzer, *Nation's Blood Resource*.

6. Minutes of Board of Governors, American Red Cross, February 15, 1971.

7. Correspondence of George M. Elsey, president, American National Red Cross, and Bernice M. Hemphill, president, American Association of Blood Banks, between

April 19, 1976, and May 3, 1976; and subsequent letters and memorandums by Robert G. Wick, vice-president, American National Red Cross.

8. Letters of Lewellys F. Barker, vice-president, American Red Cross, to William D. Dolan, president, American Blood Commission, March 1, 1983; and of Richard Landfield, Landfield, Becker and Green, counsel to the American Blood Resources Association, to Michael H. Cardozo, counsel to the American Blood Commission, May 3, 1983.

A Note on the Book

This book was edited by
Gertrude Kaplan and Elizabeth Ashooh.
Pat Taylor designed the cover.
The text was set in Palatino, a
typeface designed by Hermann Zapf.
Harper Graphics of Waldorf, Maryland
set the type, and R.R. Donnelley & Sons
Company, of Harrisonburg, Virginia
printed and bound the book, using
permanent, acid-free paper made by
the S.D. Warren Company

SELECTED AEI PUBLICATIONS

Incentives vs. Controls in Health Policy: Broadening the Debate, Jack A. Meyer, ed. (1985, 156 pp., cloth $15.95, paper $7.95)

Medicaid Reform: Four Studies of Case Management, Deborah A. Freund, with Polly M. Ehrenhaft and Marie Hackbarth (1984, 83 pp., paper $5.95)

Managing Health Care Costs: Private Sector Innovations, Sean Sullivan, ed., with Polly M. Ehrenhaft (1984, 106 pp., cloth $15.95, paper $7.95)

Controlling Medicaid Costs: Federalism, Competition, and Choice, Thomas W. Grannemann and Mark V. Pauly (1983, 112 pp., cloth $13.95, paper $4.95)

Passing the Health Care Buck: Who Pays the Hidden Cost? Jack A. Meyer, with William R. Johnson and Sean Sullivan (1983, 49 pp., $3.95)

Competition in the Pharmaceutical Industry: The Declining Profitability of Drug Innovation, Meir Statman (1983, 84 pp., $4.95)

Economics and Medical Research, Burton A. Weisbrod (1983, 171 pp., cloth $15.95, paper $7.95)

Market Reforms in Health Care: Current Issues, New Directions, Strategic Decisions, Jack A. Meyer, ed. (1983, 331 pp., cloth $19.95, paper $10.95)

Meeting Human Needs: Toward a New Public Philosophy, Jack A. Meyer, ed. (1982, 469 pp., cloth $34.95, paper $13.95)

AEI ASSOCIATES PROGRAM